The language of success

.elow. (
book

Other titles in the series

Raising the standard
Addressing the needs of gifted and talented pupils (NPF1)
Anneli McLachlan

Impact on learning
What ICT can bring to MFL in KS3 (NPF3)
Claire Dugard & Sue Hewer

CILT, the National Centre for Languages, seeks to support
and develop multilingualism and intercultural competence
among all sectors of the population in the UK.

CILT is a registered charity, supported by Central
Government grants.

NEW PATHFINDER

The language of success

Improving grades at GCSE

2

DAVE CARTER

The views expressed in this publication are the author's and do not necessarily represent those of CILT.

First published 2003 by the Centre for Information on Language Teaching and Research (CILT), 20 Bedfordbury, London WC2N 4LB

Illustration (p51) by Richard Duszczak

ISBN 1 904243 14 2

A catalogue record for this book is available from the British Library

Printed in Great Britain by Hobbs

CILT Publications are available from: **Central Books,** 99 Wallis Rd, London E9 5LN. Tel: 0845 458 9910. Fax: 0845 458 9912. On-line orders: www.centralbooks.co.uk. Book trade representation (UK and Ireland): **Broadcast Book Services,** Charter House, 29a London Rd, Croydon CR0 2RE. Tel: 020 8681 8949. Fax: 020 8688 0615.

contents

Introduction

The language of success demonstrates the precise language skills, learning strategies and techniques that students will require in order to do well in the new GCSE, coupled with suggestions about how students can acquire and practise them.

This *New Pathfinder* looks at:

- **helping** your students acquire the vocabulary they will need in the exam, and preparing them to cope when they meet a word they don't know;
- **encouraging** your students to use the grammar and structures they know to best effect in the exam;
- **preparing** your students for each of the four skills, including coursework, with examples and sample answers;
- **good exam practice**, including practical tips on exam techniques for students, and for teachers in the Speaking test.

It does not assume that all students are highly motivated, nor that teachers have infinite amounts of time, but concentrates on a down-to-earth and realistic approach to improving GCSE success.

Although students will need to have much the same skills and knowledge as before, there are changes in emphasis in the new GCSE criteria which will have an impact on the way these aspects are tested.

The new criteria

Withdrawal of dictionaries from external assessment

Most teachers – and students – will see this as the most significant change in the new GCSE. This book will consider ways in which students can be encouraged and helped to learn new vocabulary, as well as strategies which will help them when they **do** meet unknown words.

Grammar and structures

While there are some changes to the grammatical content of GCSE – mainly the requirement for both Foundation and Higher Tier candidates to be able to manipulate a wider range of verb tenses – these will not significantly alter the general appearance of the examination papers, but we will look at ways in which students at most levels can use a range of structures in order to maximise their marks.

ICT

As far as assessment is concerned, the requirement for students to use ICT skills to support their learning has its most obvious impact on the production of coursework assignments, and reference will be made to some of the benefits – and pitfalls – this can have for students. Reading papers will also increasingly reflect the spread of electronic communications, and will feature material from both websites and e-mail. This change can be considered largely cosmetic, however, since the content of the communication will still be within the structures and topics of the specifications. There is no doubt that the greatest impact of ICT will be in the range and accessibility of up-to-date texts and information in the foreign language which the teacher can find or make available for the student.

Knowledge and accurate application of grammar and structures

In the different Specifications, marks are awarded under this heading for Use of Language (the ability to use a range of structures and vocabulary) and Accuracy (the extent to which these structures are applied correctly). The criteria for assessment may have different names for these notions, but all the Specifications must allocate at least 10% of the total mark to this area. In the Writing and Speaking chapters we will consider ways of helping candidates achieve highly in these areas.

This book will focus on what the teacher and the student can do to meet the challenges of the new GCSE, concentrating first on the acquisition of the necessary **knowledge**, then on its **application** in the different parts of the examination, and ending with suggestions which will help students with the techniques required to put the language they have acquired to best use in the exam itself.

Who this book is aimed at

While the book may appear to be targeted at students and teachers in Years 10 and 11, success at GCSE depends on the development of good practice throughout the foreign language course, from the beginning of Year 7 or earlier. Indeed, much can be learnt from strategies used by students in learning their own language from the very beginning of formal schooling, in particular through the National Literacy Strategy.

The book is intended to help students **at all** levels to maximise their GCSE grade. It almost goes without saying that there is a direct correlation between a student's final grade and his or her motivation, but it is hoped that some of the ideas in this book will actually increase motivation for weaker students by giving them some simple and immediate tips for (relative) exam success, without too much effort on their part. Grade A students, on the other hand, who are probably not too lacking in motivation, will benefit from the focus on making the best use of their knowledge in the exam. The main body of students, who lie somewhere between these two extremes, including the borderline D/C students about whom many thousands of words have already been written, will benefit from the ideas about almost painless language learning **and** from the advice on how to use their limited knowledge of the language to jump through the various examination hoops more effectively.

The checklists on pp19, 38, 39, 47, 50, 51, 65, 83, 84, 86 and 87 are photocopiable for classroom use.

Words

chapter 1

How do students acquire vocabulary?

Active acquisition

The new GCSE Specifications all contain a Minimum Core vocabulary for Foundation Tier. This contains all the words which Foundation Tier candidates are expected to know. The Speaking and Writing tests will not require them to use any words outside the list, and the Listening and Reading tests will not target words which do not appear in the list, though particularly in Reading, passages aimed at Grade C may contain further vocabulary.

It is clearly to candidates' advantage, therefore, to learn as many as possible of the words in this list. Since the list for each Specification typically contains between 1500 and 2000 words, specifically targeting all these words could involve students being asked to learn upwards of 30 words per week throughout their GCSE course – with the apparently inevitable testing that this would involve – in addition to all the structures they will need. Not only would such an approach relegate the learning of a foreign language to sheer drudgery even for the best students, but teachers are fully aware that it is ineffective for the very students who need it most. How many words are known on the Friday of the test, only to disappear forever during the ensuing weekend? It is also a very crude form of learning, which tends to emphasise spelling and the written form at the expense of pronunciation. What then are the alternatives?

• Build on the students' own knowledge. Most of our students have been studying the language for as much as three years before embarking on their GCSE course. When approaching the vocabulary needed for a particular topic, get **them** to brainstorm the words they already know. For instance, even if they have not covered staying in a hotel, they should between them be able to come up with at least: *une chambre; un lit; une salle de bains; une douche; la salle à manger; la télé; le petit déjeuner; le déjeuner; le dîner.* Many of those (and there will of course be some) who could remember few of these words for themselves will learn at least a few more because they have been actively involved in the production of the list. Of course, there will be a number of words required by the topic which the students have not produced from memory. So move on to the next step.

- Complete the list by presenting the remaining words in context. With extracts from hotel brochures (realia, or from the coursebook, or made up for the purpose) encourage the students to fill in the gaps in the required vocabulary, either with the help of their dictionary, or by using one of the strategies shown in the next section.
- Encourage students to keep a vocabulary notebook in which they note new words (see Pathfinder 34, Chapter 3). These can also be used to reinforce gender (by colour-coding, for example). However, with less able students, the time required to check and correct the accuracy of the content of the notebook might be counter-productive.
- Consolidate the vocabulary by encouraging its use in play. There are innumerable vocabulary games, from simple wordsearches, through filling in the missing vowels/consonants, to more complicated anagrams and sorting games. Many other word-learning games are suggested in Pathfinder 34: *Words* (Snow 1998: 18–19), including **Bingo/Loto** (played as a whole class). Played in its traditional form this is an excellent game for practising hearing and understanding numbers. It can easily be graded in difficulty to suit the level of the learner: 'On your blank grid write down any five numbers between one and ten' or 'any number between 30 and 60' or 'Write down five numbers each including a five or each including a four', etc. (Of course, the teacher may wish to use the target language for these instructions.) Bingo/Loto can also be a useful way of practising those words which are more likely to be needed for the receptive skills than the productive skills. In this case, the words would be printed on the bingo grid instead of numbers.

There is almost no limit to these games, but one thing is constant. It is almost always more effective for students to **create** the puzzles themselves than simply to **solve** your puzzles. Many more words are likely to stick in the mind of a student who has struggled to make a dozen 'hotel' words fit a ten by ten grid – and many hours of teacher time are also saved! The really important thing about games is that they are fun, so don't kill them by saying 'And tomorrow, there'll be a test on hotel vocabulary. Detention for anyone who gets less than six out of ten!' Some words will stick, some won't – but then the same is true of 'traditional' formal learning and testing.

There are a number of published vocabulary books which contain listings of GCSE words, e.g. Nelson Thornes – *Vocabulary for GCSE* (French – Horsfall and Crossland 2001; German and Spanish versions also available); Hodder & Stoughton – *Mot à mot*

(Humberstone 2000; German and Spanish versions also available). The *GCSE vocabulary learning toolkits* (Carter 2001 – French and Brammall 2001 – German) feature a variety of vocabulary-acquisition games.

If you still have a sneaking feeling that foreign language learning should include some learning by students of lists of words, ask yourself some questions first:

- Do the students need to know the correctly spelt written form of the words? (Testing often assumes that this is the most important – or even only – criterion for success.)
- Do the students know **how** to set about learning a list of words? Is 'look – cover – write – check' sufficient, or should it be 'look – copy – cover – write – check'? It probably depends on the individual student. Encourage students to try different methods until they find one which suits them.
- How much time does the whole process take?
- Does it work? If you have two similar groups (in terms of ability and motivation), try giving each group a reading test which targets the relevant vocabulary (a much more valid test than asking them to reproduce the list) – but only specifically telling one of the groups to learn the words for homework. Compare the results.

(See also Chapter 3 – How can students cope with gender and agreement?)

Passive acquisition

Knowledge of the vocabulary content of the Specifications is so crucial to success that it cannot be left to chance, and a systematic approach to acquiring this vocabulary such as that outlined above is essential. However, this approach contains elements of the 'passivity' with which mature language learners acquire vocabulary, in that it gets away from the more traditional 'read – remember – test' routine which is often unsuccessful, and will lead to at least some new vocabulary being learnt by even those students who are unwilling to invest time and effort in this area.

However, in the new GCSE candidates, particularly at the higher levels, are expected to use appropriately 'a wide range of vocabulary ...' (AQA Speaking and Writing criteria at about the A/A* area), and even around Grade C candidates need to show 'some variety in the use of vocabulary' (ibid). Clearly, therefore, knowledge of vocabulary beyond that which is defined by the syllabus is valuable, not only in the active skills, but also in Listening and Reading, where a more wide-ranging vocabulary is likely to be met, if not specifically targeted. It must be said here that the awarding bodies publish in one form or another a 'suggested' Higher Tier vocabulary. The status of this is not absolutely clear, but it would be wise for teachers entering students for Higher papers to ensure that they are aware of this 'extra' vocabulary, not least because, although it is not statutory, question-setters will inevitably have it very much in mind when setting questions.

Even beyond this, however, there is a vocabulary which the teacher cannot, and would probably not wish to, prescribe, since to do so would remove the essentially individual nature of language learning, and it is in this area of personal interest where passive vocabulary acquisition is perhaps most important. Students at all levels can be given the opportunity to read in the target language about things which interest them. In addition to reading libraries, the Internet provides a wealth of information about every imaginable topic. If the school has access to the World Wide Web, most students are capable (with a certain amount of judicious supervision!) of entering a key word in a search at (for example) **fr@yahoo.com**, and retrieving information about their favourite French footballer. Even without any conscious effort, some of the vocabulary they meet will stay with them because of their own interest.

Acquisition of new vocabulary is much more likely to result from reading than from listening, especially in those languages in which the sound of a word is more often a barrier than an aid to comprehension – in French, for example, there are many cognates or near-cognates in the written language, but almost none in the spoken language. This means that care needs to be taken:

- to reinforce the **sound** of newly-acquired vocabulary;
- to ensure that testing, where this is done, is done through the appropriate medium, which is often not writing, where the emphasis is inevitably on correct spelling. For example, it makes little sense to test the spelling of numbers greater than nine – and arguably of any numbers.

Using the dictionary

Although students are not allowed to use their dictionary in the exam, the dictionary is an invaluable tool in the acquisition of vocabulary, though training is needed in its effective use. Apart from the mechanics of dictionary use, which will certainly need to be taught with reference to a bilingual dictionary (but hopefully not in Years 10 or 11) there are probably two important lessons to be learnt about using the dictionary. First of all, students should be encouraged to use it sparingly, since intensive dictionary use removes any spontaneity in reading. Secondly, they need to use the English to target language section with even greater care, bearing in mind that if they look up 'nut' they will find *Nuss, Schraubenmutter* and *Verrückte*, and that the wrong choice will make a very strange sentence. Willing students can be encouraged, when they look up a word in their dictionary, to look also at the word before or after it. If they look up twenty words a week, and if only a quarter of the extra words stick in their memory, they will acquire 'free' twenty words a month.

It is worth giving some thought to the type of dictionary which is best for GCSE students. While a very small format is easy to carry around, it may not be very user-friendly in terms of layout, and the small print can make it harder to follow the examples. A very 'GCSE-focused' dictionary may not allow better students to develop the range of vocabulary they are capable of, and will not be of much value if they go on to further study. A dictionary which is too large, on the other hand, risks confusing GCSE students with its wealth of examples, and inclusion perhaps of archaic or slang forms. For most students, a dictionary which is designed for GCSE students, but not in an over-limited fashion, will probably be the best choice – accessible enough to use every day, but not simplistic.

See also Pathfinder 28: *Making effective use of the dictionary* (Berwick and Horsfall 1996).

Although GCSE questions in all skills are designed to test knowledge of grammar and structures, the importance of vocabulary cannot be stressed too much. It is probably true that in the passive skills, more marks are 'lost' by candidates at all levels because they do not know or recognise a particular word than because of any lack of understanding of structures. In Speaking and Writing, candidates normally have a certain amount of choice in what they say, so they are often able to conceal any vocabulary gaps – if you've forgotten the Spanish for 'cat', say you've got a dog! However, some tasks (most role plays, and many writing tasks – such as a letter to a hotel booking a room) do require a specific vocabulary, and ignorance of it will make completion of the task impossible.

How can they cope with unknown words?

Word patterns

The new GCSE criteria refer to 'knowledge and accurate application of the grammar and structures of the language', and students should be made aware of the fact that included in the structures of a language are the patterns which are followed by individual words. Many of these (such as verb conjugations) are among the difficulties of a foreign language for English speakers, but there are many word patterns which can be of great value in recognising words which have not been met before:

- The ability to recognise and isolate prefixes and suffixes (in a number of languages many of these are similar to their English equivalent) can reduce a long and complex word to its more easily recognisable stem:
  *un*verzeihlich = **un**forgiv**able**
- Some of these patterns are so regular that better students can even use them to form their own words:
  -eur/euse = someone who does (*footballeur*);
  -ier = tree the fruit grows on (*poirier*)
- A few simple exercises from time to time to develop students' ability to make use of these word patterns in their reading will not only increase their vocabulary, but will give them more confidence, as they will not panic so easily when confronted with a strange word.
- Like strategies for acquiring vocabulary, techniques for coping with unknown words tend to concentrate on the written form, but awareness of the sounds which go with certain letter combinations can greatly help in understanding. In French *champion* is a perfect cognate in its written form, but far from a cognate when it is heard; it is only when the hearer is aware of the letter combinations which form the sounds *cham* and *ion* that any similarity with English can be identified.

Context and intelligent guesswork

All too often, candidates at GCSE fail to apply what they know about real life in their struggle to cope with the foreign language. When they hear that the price of an ice cream is *ein Euro fünfzig*, they are so grateful to have understood *fünfzig* that they give the price as €50, although they must be aware that a £30 ice-cream would really be something special.

If students read that 'the man had a large X on a lead', and they don't recognise 'X', then it's worth going with the most likely guess – that it's some sort of dog. This may seem obvious, but students often don't make the link between what they read in the foreign language and reality, and unless they are trained to approach texts methodically and calmly, will often simply panic before an unknown – or forgotten – word.

key points	• Always start from words which the candidate already knows.
	• Introduce new words in context.
	• Remember – games are for fun! Students will find some gain, without feeling any pain!
	• Students need reading material which interests them – for example, on the Internet.
	• Teach word patterns as well as individual words.
	• Common sense rules OK! Logic can help understand a new word almost as much as a dictionary.

Sentences

☐ How can students be encouraged to produce
   sentences?

☐ How can they make their sentences longer?
   (Grades F to D)
   - Adjectives and adverbs
   - Linking words
   - Phrases

☐ How can they make their sentences more
   complex? (Grades C to A*)
   - Subordinate clauses

chapter 2

Although there are clear differences between the sort of language used in writing and that produced in speaking, it is a general principle that progress up the assessment criteria will reflect the length and complexity of the utterances produced by the student. A student operating at Grade G will communicate through single words and short phrases, with an occasional pre-learnt sentence. Attempts to produce sentences will usually reproduce the prompt or stimulus, often failing because of anglicised vocabulary and sentence structure. A student operating at Grade C will produce simple sentences of the subject – verb – complement type, with some attempts to link two sentences, and to add extra details. A student operating at Grade A will communicate mainly in linked sentences, showing a range of structures, and depending relatively little on the stimulus. Naturally, within these broad descriptors, accuracy will determine the effectiveness and quality of the communication (see Chapter 3).

In both Speaking and Writing, the Grade Description for Grade A requires candidates to 'produce longer sequences', while the criteria for assessment use descriptors such as 'Offers some examples of subordination' (Edexcel Speaking), 'Some variety of clause types, e.g. subordinate clauses' (OCR Written coursework), or '… attempts at longer sentences using appropriate linking words' (AQA Writing) at around the Grade C/B threshold.

The transition from word-level to sentence-level is explored further in Young Pathfinder 9: *The literacy link* (Cheater and Farren 2001).

How can students be encouraged to produce sentences?

Students should not be discouraged from giving very brief, one-word responses to questions or tasks, as these may be both natural and very communicative. Rather, a student's own short answer should be treated as the first stage in developing a more complete answer. If a student's answer to the question 'What is your favourite subject?' is 'Games', he or she can be encouraged to turn this into a fuller answer ('Imagine you hadn't been asked the question. How would you tell someone that your favourite subject is Games?'). Again, this could be done as a whole-class activity using the 'magic slate' (see later in this chapter).

Games can then be played to build on the initial sentence. 'How many different sentences can we make by changing the name of the school subject?' At a higher level, the question could become 'How many different sentences can we make by changing the verb?' If this approach to sentence-building is used regularly, students will gradually become aware of sentence structure, and of the possibilities of word substitution as a means of creating a bank of language to fit different situations. Even inappropriate substitutions (when talking about school subjects, substituting the verb to eat, instead of to prefer or to dislike) also serve to reinforce the basic sentence structure, as long as the spirit of competition remains friendly rather than aggressive.

How can they make their sentences longer?

If we take the basic means of communication as the simple sentence (subject, verb, complement) then anything which adds to this is producing longer sequences. This can be done in a number of very simple ways:

- by the addition of one or more words, such as:
  - an adjective:
    Tengo un hermano. ➡ *Tengo un hermano **mayor**.*
  - or an adverb:
    J'aime le français. ➡ *J'aime **beaucoup** le français.*
  - or turning a single item into a list using 'and':
    Ich habe einen Hund. ➡ *Ich habe einen Hund **und** eine Katze.*
- by putting together two or more basic sentences using a linking word:
  J'aime le français. Je déteste les maths. ➡ *J'aime le français **mais** je déteste les maths.*
  I ate my breakfast. I left the house. ➡ I ate my breakfast, **then** I left the house.

From the point of view of students working at Grade D, these techniques have the great advantage that they meet the assessment criteria beyond grade D **without** requiring any greater grammatical knowledge – clearly the use of an adjective requires awareness of gender, but no more than the almost unavoidable use of an article in the more basic sentence. This, like many of the other points made in this book, may seem to involve simply performing certain pre-learnt tricks in order to score higher marks in the exam, and to have little to do with extending students' ability to use the language. However, the criteria merely reflect general perceptions of what constitute advanced language skills, and there is no doubt that length of sentence, in the native language as in a foreign language, is one of the key indicators of increasing expertise.

From a relatively early stage in learning the foreign language, simple writing frames which encourage the use of adjectives and adverbs, as well as sentence-linking, can be used to good effect. Such writing frames also encourage students to be aware of relationships such as contrast and sequence within their writing and speaking. The use of writing frames is considered in depth in Pathfinder 40: *Just write!* (Adams and Panter 2001).

1	2	3
J'aime la musique classique		Je n'aime pas les films policiers
Je joue au tennis		Je quitte la maison
Je mange les légumes	et	Je me couche
Je suis beau/belle		Je regarde la télé
J'aime les films westerns		Je mange les fruits
Je regarde la télé	mais	Je joue aux échecs
Je suis intelligent(e)		Je suis intelligent(e)
Je mange le petit déjeuner		Je ne mange pas la viande
Je fais mes devoirs	puis	Je n'aime pas la musique rock
Je joue au rugby		Je prends ma douche

This sort of exercise can be made more exciting if the teacher or a member of the class selects a sentence from columns 1 and 3, and the rest of the class produces the appropriate link word. Whole-class activities of this kind can be made to involve every individual member of the class by the use of that old-fashioned student resource, the slate, or in its more up-to-date form the 'magic slate', where words can be written using a stylus, then erased simply by lifting the clear plastic sheet. (Thanks for this idea to Catherine Cheater, Language Teaching Adviser, CILT.) Words can be quickly written down, held up for the teacher and the rest of the class to see, and then as quickly removed. This will reinforce understanding of the basic sentences, and of the relationships imposed by the different link words, and because it is an activity which doesn't put the individual on the spot, will encourage understanding of the concepts by weaker members of the class without any explicit grammatical awareness. Beware! If this exercise produces lots of giggles, one of the class may be holding up the slate backwards for his or her mates to read the rude words he or she has written!

- by adding quite simple adjectival or adverbial phrases to a basic sentence:
  *Mon frère est grand **aux yeux bleus***. My brother is tall **with blue eyes.**

Again, these structures, although superficially more complex than single adjectives or adverbs, can often consist of extra, often quite basic, vocabulary, and students should be encouraged to add at least some to everything they say and write. This may begin as a purely mechanical hoop to jump through, but if it can be encouraged to the point at which it becomes second nature to expand on basic sentences, the linguistic level of the student will have moved up a level.

How can they make their sentences more complex?

Although there are a number of ways in which students can produce more complex sentences, such as using a wider variety of verb tenses within sentences or using direct speech, the one descriptor of complexity to which the assessment criteria of all the examining groups refer is the ability to use subordinate clauses. Subordinate clauses themselves vary in their degree of complexity, from those which simply require the use of certain conjunctions (when; where; because) which may have no grammatical consequences, to relative pronouns, the correct use of which may require some grammatical knowledge, to structures like the French *bien que* or *quoique*, which are followed by the subjunctive. It is fair to say that the use of subordinate clauses with confidence can only be achieved by the best students, though, as is the case with adding extra details to produce longer sentences, students at round about Grade D can be successfully encouraged to mechanically include one or two subordinate clauses in any longer piece of writing.

It is worth considering giving students a list of useful structures, such as the one at the end of this chapter, for producing longer and more complex sentences, and encouraging them to use at least some of them (the number could vary according to the level of the student, as could the words/structures included – to facilitate this, they are arranged in approximate order of complexity) in every piece of written work. (See also Grade A and Grade C Checklists in Chapter 7. German and Spanish versions of the list of useful structures are given in the appendix.)

It may be felt that students who normally operate at around Grade A, and who are capable of internalising these structures as they appear, do not really need the support of such mechanistic training. However, as all teachers of modern languages know, there is an enormous gulf between what our best students **know**, and what they actually **use** in their work, especially in exams. A checklist will at least serve to remind them of what the examiner is looking for, and used regularly when producing work will keep the need to use complex structures at the front of the students' minds.

Such an approach is much more appropriate in writing, and indeed many of the more complex structures referred to in this chapter are less likely to be used in speaking. However, students do need to be made aware of the need to add extra details and use longer utterances in speaking too, though it is clearly natural to make greater use of less complex language.

key points	• **Even at a very basic level, students need to be encouraged to add a bit extra.**
	• **Reinforce language patterns by using mechanical models such as the grid shown under 'How can they make their sentences longer?' and pre-learnt phrases.**
	• **Encourage students to use checklists to make sure they have included more complex structures.**
	• **Stress the need for greater length and complexity in speaking as well as writing.**

Making longer sentences

et – and
*Je regarde la télé **et** je fais mes devoirs.*

mais – but
*Je voudrais aller au cinéma **mais** je n'ai pas d'argent.*

puis – then
*J'ai fait mes devoirs **puis** je me suis couché(e).*

ensuite – next
*D'abord je me lave, **ensuite** je prends le petit déjeuner.*

qui – who
*J'ai un frère **qui** s'appelle John.*

où – where
*J'habite une ville **où** il y a beaucoup à faire.*

quand – when
***Quand** j'ai du temps libre, j'aime écouter de la musique.*

pendant que – while
*Je bavarde avec mes amis **pendant que** je mange mes sandwichs.*

parce que – because
*J'aime la géo **parce que** le prof est sympa.*

ce qui – what
***Ce qui** m'intéresse au collège, c'est l'histoire.*

ce que – what
***Ce que** j'aime faire, c'est passer mes vacances à l'étranger.*

avant de – before
*Je range ma chambre **avant de** sortir avec mes copines.*

P © CILT 2003

après avoir – after
***Après avoir** mangé, je fais la vaisselle.*

puisque – since
***Puisque** nous allons en ville, je vais acheter des vêtements.*

si – if
*J'irai au cinéma la semaine prochaine, **si** j'ai assez d'argent.*

bien que – although
***Bien que** j'aime le football, je ne vais pas souvent aux matchs.*

---

très – very
d'habitude/en général/généralement/ normalement – normally
aussi – also
enfin – at last
(mal)heureusement – (un)fortunately
tout d'un coup – suddenly
souvent – often
par contre – on the other hand
pourtant/cependant – however
d'une part ... d'autre part – on the one hand ... on the other hand
presque – almost
bientôt – soon
plus tard – later
assez – quite/fairly
tout à fait – completely
finalement – finally
d'ailleurs – besides
tout de suite – immediately
c'est-à-dire – that is to say
par exemple – for example
également – also
et ainsi de suite – and so on

Grammar

chapter 3

☐ What is new about grammar in the new GCSE?

☐ How can students cope with gender and agreement?

☐ How important are verbs and tenses?

☐ What role does grammar play in comprehension?

☐ How can we practise grammar?

What is new about grammar in the new GCSE?

In terms of the grammar and linguistic structures which appear in all the new Specifications, the changes obviously vary from one examining group to another – depending on what the content of the previous syllabus was – but are relatively insignificant. Although, for example, the pluperfect tense and the passive voice are now referred to at Foundation Tier, for receptive use, it may not seem either necessary or appropriate to introduce these verb forms to a lower-achieving set, for whom grammatical markers rarely impinge on comprehension. Similarly at Higher Tier, the pluperfect tense may have moved from receptive to active use, but we do not need to put any greater emphasis on this tense than was previously the case, since it is (and was) the case that using the pluperfect forms part of the armoury which a top-level student might have at his or her disposal in demonstrating the ability to use a variety of structures. It is hard to imagine that there will be many tasks in the new writing exams which will **oblige** the use of the pluperfect.

The difference in the new Specifications is in the new emphasis on accuracy, range and complexity in the assessment criteria. While a candidate at Higher Tier may not **be obliged** by the tasks to use the comparative, direct and indirect object pronouns, the conditional, imperfect and pluperfect tenses, the perfect infinitive and the present participle, he or she will probably not progress to the top of the assessment criteria without using at least some of them, both in speaking and in writing.

How can students cope with gender and agreement?

There is no easy way of dealing with this problem. For native speakers of English, gender is unfamiliar ground, and students find it hard to be consistently accurate. Though there are sometimes 'rules', many of them have an exception rate of 20% or more, which makes them very unreliable. Strategies such as using colour-coding or separate columns in vocabulary notebooks may be quite effective for some students, but the most effective way of learning gender is always to learn a new noun together with an adjective. There is evidence to suggest that young native-speaker children easily acquire gender because they enjoy detailed descriptions in the stories which are read to them and later which they read for themselves, and therefore the sentences they hear and see are full of gender markers. It therefore makes sense, when practising newly acquired vocabulary, for the teacher to make every effort to include in exercises and questions as many grammatical markers as possible. In French, for example, it is very tempting to use, and encourage students to use, the form of question which relies simply on intonation (*La voiture est rouge?*), since this requires the least grammatical manipulation on the part of the student. However, using the 'est-ce que' form (*La voiture, est-ce qu'elle est rouge?*) contains two gender markers, one of which (the use of *'elle'*) is much stronger than the simple definite article (Surridge 1995).

Clearly, with gender as with any other grammatical concept, it is important to teach correctness, and to encourage accuracy. As always, however, the emphasis we give to accuracy varies in correlation to the ability of the students. While frequent use of wrong gender would conflict with the 'generally accurate' descriptor for Grade A work, isolated mistakes would constitute 'minor errors', that is, generally, errors which do not impede communication, and would not in themselves preclude the achievement of a high grade. Similarly, a student could make a number of gender errors, and still get a Grade C. With students below this level, it is important to concentrate most of our attention on major errors such as inappropriate vocabulary or structures which obscure or distort meaning.

How important are verbs and tenses?

Students operating below Grade D

The present tense

This is invariably the first tense to be taught, and is generally the main tense targeted by tasks and prompts in both writing and speaking, in addition to being the main tense used in listening and reading items, especially at Foundation Tier. This should not obscure the fact that it is also often the most difficult tense to learn, and probably has the largest number of irregular forms. This is not to say that we can skimp on our teaching of the present tense to weaker students, but that perhaps we should encourage them in greater use of other tenses – particularly compound tenses where the structure of the verb is more predictable – rather than focusing all our efforts on fixing the present tense in their minds.

At this level, most of the students' active use of language will be in the first person singular. It is worth giving them a list of the most common question form of the (twenty) most common verbs, and encouraging them to respond automatically with the first person singular of the appropriate verb, so that, for instance, hearing or seeing a question containing *'aimez-vous'* will trigger a response containing *'j'aime'*. In this way, the correct verb form becomes a lexical rather than a grammatical response.

A past tense

A similar approach can be used with whatever is the most usual past tense (depending on the language). Although the grade descriptions do not expect students below Grade C to be able to refer to different time frames, if as is often the case the past is 'easier' than the present, its use can enhance the accuracy and range of language score even of weaker students.

Students operating at about Grade C

In addition to the above:

A future reference

In many languages, reference to the future can appropriately be made without using a different tense – for example, in German by using the present tense (*Heute Abend gehe ich ins Kino*), or in French by using *'aller'* with the infinitive, or the present tense with an appropriate future marker (*Ce soir, je vais au cinéma*). If this is the case, the Grade C grade description ('Candidates write about … , including past present and future events and involving the use of different tenses') can be met by effective use of present and past tenses.

Students operating at Grade B and above

These students will be expected to use the tenses referred to above with some confidence; they will therefore need to have internalised the necessary verb formations, rather than using the sort of programmed responses mentioned above.

In the past tense, students will need to give descriptions and accounts, which may involve the use of a different past tense. For all but the best students, it may be appropriate to give them a bank of descriptive sentences which they can use as appropriate to the topic, for example, in French, a range of imperfect sentences such as:

- *Il/Elle était* + a range of adjectives;
- *Il faisait* + weather expressions.

The best students might also be encouraged to include a pluperfect tense to increase the range and complexity of their language.

In the future, students can be encouraged to include a conditional (possibly with an 'if' clause) to add variety, if the topic lends itself to this.

At this level, it is important that candidates are aware of the necessity to use a **wide range** of structures in order to obtain the best marks.

What role does grammar play in comprehension?

If it is true that most marks in Foundation Tier listening and reading tests are gained by recognition of individual words or short phrases, it is equally true that the Higher Tier papers will require some grammatical understanding.

Tense: answers may require students to distinguish between past, present and future.

Negation: many marks are lost (especially in Listening) by students who fail to pick out a negative expression.

Gist: students need to be aware that at Higher Tier, many of the questions will require them to understand the overall message of a passage, and that relying on a key word or phrase will very often let them down.

How can we practise grammar?

Build on what has already been done

Since the introduction of the National Literacy Strategy, more and more frequently students enter their first MFL lesson with an awareness of at least the basic grammatical vocabulary such as noun, verb, adjective, adverb. We can therefore talk about sentence structure without the necessity to explain our terms.

Use lots of class games and activities such as substitution exercises to reinforce the grammatical function of certain types of words without putting individual students on the spot. If we want students to be willing to try new ways of expressing themselves, and to be creative in their use of the foreign language, we need to use methods which do not dent their self-confidence. This approach can be used even with top sets in the initial stages of learning even quite complex structures. Here are just a few examples:

- To practise the comparative, each student prepares cards with the words *'plus'*, *'aussi'* and *'moins'*. The teacher then shows on the OHP or the board a cartoon illustrating the appropriate comparison, and a sentence with a missing word, e.g. cartoon shows girl saying '2 + 2 = 4', and boy saying '2 + 2 = 5'. Sentence reads: *Jean est ... intelligent que Marie.* Students hold up card showing *'moins'*.

- A similar approach could be used to practise verb endings for a new tense. Students prepare cards as above showing the relevant verb endings. The teacher prepares a series of sentences showing only the stem of the verb: as each sentence is revealed, students hold up the appropriate ending.

As soon as possible, get students to use the new grammar for their own purposes. Rather than telling them what you want them to say, ask them what they could use the new structure to express.

Encourage students to play with newly-acquired structures. Silly sentences will stick in the mind for much longer than sensible – but boring – ones: 'If I was rich I would live in a cardboard box'.

Get the level right

To take a simple example, if you have a bottom set, they might well meet the future tense in their coursebook, but it may not be worth spending too much time in learning how it works – at least not for exam purposes. If they meet a future in the exam – unlikely at Foundation – it helps if they can recognise the verb, but the fact that it is in the future won't usually affect their understanding.

key points	• Use structures which emphasise and reinforce gender.
	• References to past, present and future are essential for Grade C students – make sure they include them in every piece of written work, and all extended speaking.
	• Students beyond Grade C need to use a range of tenses, not just the minimum three time frames.
	• At Higher Tier listening and reading, students can't assume that identification of key words/phrases will be enough.
	• Encourage students to use new grammar for their own purposes, whether serious or fun.

Speaking

☐ What can be done to reduce the level of stress in the Speaking test?

☐ How can students improve their pronunciation?

☐ What is the best way to tackle role plays?

☐ How can students use pre-prepared material to best effect?

☐ What should students (and teachers) do in the Conversation?

chapter 4

What can be done to reduce the level of stress in the Speaking test?

The foreign language speaking test is, for many students, the most stressful event of their school lives. For many language **teachers**, it is the most stressful time of the school year. In many ways, this is unavoidable. Students are aware that, for ten or twelve minutes, they are going to reveal the extent of their knowledge or ignorance, and unlike in a written test, which will be seen only by an anonymous examiner, their teacher will hear every word. Teachers know that a good performance by the student, at whatever level, depends on how well the teacher conducts the test, particularly the conversation. Reference will be made later to techniques that both students and teachers can use to achieve maximum effectiveness, but there are some simple, practical preparations which will help to keep the stress to a minimum.

For the students

Ensure that they have as much experience as possible in recording themselves speaking the foreign language. Although most homes have a cassette recorder, it is rarely used by students to record their own voices, even in their own language. Use of the cassette recorder at home can also take the stress out of day-to-day speaking practice. Adolescents can be very self-conscious about speaking in public, and particularly about 'making fools of themselves' in front of their mates. Making speaking the foreign language less of a public experience by encouraging students to record work done at home, either alone or with a friend, can increase confidence by reassuring them that the rest of the class won't hear their errors and laugh at them.

Let them know in detail the form the test will take:

• How long will the whole test last?
• How many role plays?
• How long to prepare?
• What should they do in the Presentation (if there is one)?
• What sort of thing should they do in the Conversation?

Give them a full-scale practice as their mock exam. It is important that this is:

- organised just like the real thing;
- recorded on cassette – this can then be used for giving individual feedback;
- treated like any other mock exam – i.e. properly timetabled, with teachers and students given the appropriate amount of time to prepare and conduct the test.

For the actual exam:

- Be as calm as you are able.
- Take the time to put them at ease, explain (again) exactly what they should do, and what will happen, step by step.
- Rather than making individual appointments for students to come to the preparation room at a particular time, consider having a small 'holding group' of five or six students who are waiting to begin their preparation time. The students have time to compose themselves before beginning their preparation, rather than dashing in from a science practical, and the teacher has the reassurance of knowing that the next few candidates are ready and waiting. This system does not have to involve more supervision, since the holding group can be supervised by the same teacher who is responsible for invigilating the preparing candidate(s).
- Make sure that the supervising teacher knows exactly what the requirements are, and can help prevent any panic.

For the teacher

Plan carefully how many candidates you can fit into a session. If a session lasts for two and a half hours, it may be theoretically possible to conduct fifteen Foundation Tier tests (at about ten minutes each). However, it is hard to imagine that you will be as alert for the fifteenth candidate as you were for the first. It would be much better to schedule only eleven or twelve candidates, and give yourself time:

- for a comfort break;
- to check at the end of each test that the recording is satisfactory;
- to give a little reassurance to a nervous candidate.

Make sure that you are properly timetabled to conduct the tests, and are not expected to lose all your non-contact time for the week, or even worse, to fit the tests into your 'free' periods. This is equally true for mock exams.

Try as far as possible to predict, and eliminate, likely problems:

- Can you get the bell stopped while speaking tests are on?
- Can you check if there are plans to cut the grass outside the exam rooms/deliver coal/hold the regional athletics finals beneath the window? And if so, can you make sure they are changed?
- Is the exam room:
  - reasonably quiet?
  - quite small?
  - carpeted?
- Do other students (and staff) know that speaking tests are going on, and that it is important to move around quietly? More speaking test recordings are rendered hard to hear because of the raised voices of other teachers than by rowdy students!

Prepare the role plays, the questions on the Presentation (if any), and suitable questions for the Conversation in advance, so that you are comfortable with them. It may be a good idea to do this advance preparation as a departmental activity, so that everyone can benefit from the good ideas of their colleagues – especially teachers who have little or no experience of conducting speaking tests.

How can students improve their pronunciation?

Encouraging good pronunciation is clearly something which starts from the very first lesson in the foreign language. Although it is probably more of a problem in some languages than in others, pronunciation is taken into account in the assessment criteria, and even at Grade C 'Errors of … pronunciation cause only occasional problems with communication' (AQA). It is received wisdom that the best way of encouraging accurate pronunciation in students is to ensure that they have a good role model in the teacher, and that as far as possible they **hear** new language before they **see** it. However, experience tells us that this often fails to produce the desired results:

- If we encourage wide reading, and treat it as one useful way of acquiring new vocabulary, then students will inevitably learn from the written form.
- If we encourage conscious learning of new vocabulary, many students will take as their starting point the written form. Often, this will affect their pronunciation, even of words which they have used orally for some time.

The basic principle remains true – the more students have the opportunity to associate a word with its sound, the more likely they are to pronounce it correctly. In some cases, it is most important that this is done in context. Take, for example, the numbers in French:

- Students first learn the numbers from one to ten orally:
  un/deux/trois/quatre/cinq/six/sept/huit/neuf/dix
- But when they actually need to use these numbers, the sound is often not exactly what they learned:
  une fille; deuz enfants; troiz heures; quat(re) fois; siz oignons

However, since the sound is inevitably more transient than the written form, it is the written form which tends to dominate students' memories, and to influence their pronunciation. It is therefore important, in addition to giving good oral models, to teach letter/sound patterns, particularly to more able students, so that they can work out for themselves the pronunciation of a word which they have only met in print.

Also, it is important to remember that good pronunciation is not simply a matter of saying individual words correctly – though it must be admitted that if we can get our Grade C students to do this, we are probably well satisfied. However, more able students should also be encouraged to consider intonation as part of pronunciation.

For those students, perhaps the majority in the case of French, for whom accurate pronunciation is hard to achieve, a few rules of thumb may help to avoid some of the more painful pronunciation problems. These are frequently a barrier to communication, especially in the more predictable elements of the test.

- In French, remember that for *-er* verbs (by far the most common group) *é* goes only on the **past** participle and that the present tense usually ends with a **silent** *e*. Often seen as a grammatical error, this is in fact usually the most disruptive of the common pronunciation problems.

- The last letter of most French words is **silent** (especially *d, r, s, t, x* and *z*) unless it is a vowel.
- Even if a word is spelt like an English word, it will still have a French/German/Spanish pronunciation. If these cognates are pronounced in such an anglicised way as to make them unintelligible, for many students there will be little communication left. It may be worth, particularly for the weakest students, specifically practising the pronunciation of common cognates or near-cognates. Words such as *'Diamant'* or *'football'*, if pronounced as their English equivalents, may be quite incomprehensible to the native speaker of German or French respectively.

What is the best way to tackle role plays?

There are three levels of role play, and each demands its own particular approach.

Foundation Tier role plays are very tightly defined. The candidate is told precisely what to say, and marks are allocated according to the extent to which the message is delivered. However, because dictionaries are no longer available during the preparation time, the tasks may seek, where possible, to avoid situations in which a candidate cannot score the marks simply because of the lack of a specific item of vocabulary. For instance, in a café, the instruction might say 'Ask for a hot drink' rather than 'Ask for a white coffee'. This means that the candidate can ask for any hot drink which he or she can remember the foreign language word for, and does not risk losing all the marks for the task because he or she has forgotten *'Kaffee mit Milch'*.

There is a danger here for less able students, who need to be trained in the phraseology of this type of question, which does **not** require them to know the German for 'hot' nor for 'drink'! Similarly, students may need to be given training in interpreting other types of question. For example, 'Ask your friend for his or her opinion of a school subject' really means: 'Say: Do you like X?'

One or more of the tasks will require the candidate to use a sentence including a verb. Generally, candidates should be encouraged to prepare responses which are full answers containing verbs – though clearly in some cases an answer can be full and appropriate without a verb. In the German example referred to above, *'Kaffee mit Milch, bitte'* is a full and appropriate response.

One of the tasks may require the candidate to ask a question. Since the question structure is often a weak point for students – partly because unless the teacher makes a point of giving them opportunities to practise, the nature of the classroom is that it is usually the teacher who asks the questions – it is worth spending some time practising **asking** those questions which are likely to come up in Foundation role plays:

- How much …?/How many …?
- What do you …?/When do you …?/Where do you …?
- What is your name?
- How old are you?
- Do you like …?
- Do you watch …/eat …?/go to …?

Foundation/Higher role plays are quite similar to Foundation role plays, though it will be more difficult to fulfil the task without using a sentence or at least a structure, such as a preposition (unless more than one piece of information is required). There will, however, be at least one unprepared task. The position of this within the overall role play may be indicated by a **!**, or by an instruction such as 'Answer the teacher's question', or the teacher may interpose the unprepared question(s) at an appropriate point in the role play.

Students should be encouraged, when they have prepared the specified tasks, to spend the remaining time considering what sort of further questions the teacher might ask. For example, at the lost-property office, the printed tasks might require the candidate to say what has been lost, where and when. There is a limited number of other questions which might be asked in this situation:

- How much is it worth?
- Describe it.
- How can I contact you?

Although there can be no guarantee that the unprepared task will be one of these, the candidate would be well advised to prepare answers to these likely questions.

Higher role plays are quite similar to Foundation/Higher role plays, except that the tasks are set in the target language. However, the nature of the tasks is likely to:

- be more open-ended – it is therefore more important for the candidate to listen to and understand what the teacher says: he or she may need to prompt you to expand on the information you have given, to add extra details, which may be necessary to score full marks;
- need more than one detail. Even if the task doesn't specify 'Give three details', full marks are not likely to be gained for a very brief answer such as 'black'!
- require a full sentence (possibly in a tense other than the present);
- involve a problem to be solved;
- include an element of negotiation. Students should be able to use a range of phrases to cope with this, e.g.:
  - Suggest alternatives ('Can I have another ...?/... a refund?').
  - Ask for more information ('When will it be ready?').
  - Ask what is going to be done ('What will you do ...?').
  - Express difficulties ('I can't ... [on Monday]/I go back home on ...').
  - Express dissatisfaction ('I am not happy!/I want to see the manager!').

The unprepared element can be 'predicted' as mentioned above.

How can students use pre-prepared material to best effect?

Most speaking tests contain some element which may be prepared by the student in advance of the exam. This may take the form of a presentation, or of a conversation topic which the student has chosen. If used appropriately, this can be a really confidence-boosting precursor to the general conversation. However, there are some possible pitfalls to be aware of:

- A student may be tempted to choose a topic which is of personal interest, but which he or she is not linguistically equipped to deal with (pollution, for example, can be quite a challenging topic in terms of vocabulary and structures) or conversely, a topic which does not really allow him or her to use a sufficiently wide range of grammar and structures (for example, many presentations on the topic of 'My family', even those done by able students, rely mainly on Year 9 language). This does not prevent the choice of a topic which the student finds interesting, but does indicate that the choice should be made in consultation with the teacher, who needs to be guided by linguistic considerations as well as those of interest and motivation.

- Similarly, since 'reference to past, present and future events' and 'justification of opinions' appear explicitly in the grade descriptions, the topic chosen should (for Grade C candidates and above) give opportunities to demonstrate these abilities.
- Students should take advantage of as much help from the teacher as the Specification allows. However, as a general rule, the degree of direction should be in inverse proportion to the ability of the student or group. For a bottom set, a very standardised approach might be most effective, while at the other end of the range, the very best students will benefit from a great degree of freedom and flexibility.
- Since most students will do much of their preparation in writing, pronunciation can suffer (see above), and the temptation to gabble can be very strong. For the presentation, students should be strongly encouraged to practise aloud, preferably recording it on cassette, so that the teacher can help with any pronunciation problems, and to observe any timings given in the specification.
- Neither the presentation nor the pre-selected topic consists entirely of a monologue by the student, and although the student needs to prepare what he or she wishes to say, he or she also needs to plan for teacher interventions. Although these may be fairly predictable, depending on the requirements of the Specification, the student needs to make sure that some areas are left for the teacher to question or ask for elucidation about. Equally, the teacher needs to have some appropriate questions to ask about the topic.

What should students (and teachers) do in the Conversation?

In this part of the Speaking test, it is the job of the candidate to use the range of vocabulary and structures of which he or she is capable. In order for the candidate to do this, the teacher must provide the candidate with appropriate opportunities.

What the teacher should do

Make sure that the student has learnt a bank of answers (together with his or her 'prompt' questions) for each of the conversation topics. On the topic of leisure, for example, these might include answers to:

- *Was machst du in deiner Freizeit?*
- *Was machst du abends?*
- *Was machst du am Wochenende?*
- *Was ist dein Lieblingshobby?*
- *Bist du sportlich?*

These are obviously very basic, but even for a very good student, they can be the starting point for a high-level conversation, while students who are less sure of themselves can gain a lot of confidence from knowing that they will have at least some of the answers ready. If the first of the series of questions contains a key word (like *Freizeit*) this will allow the student to home in on the appropriate subject area.

For the test itself, have ready a range of questions for each topic suitable for different levels of candidates. The grid showing key elements of the criteria for assessment of speaking, which appears at the end of this chapter, gives clear information about the qualities which candidates **must** demonstrate. With better candidates it is not enough simply to work through a list of questions. As far as possible within the constraints of the test, a natural conversation should be allowed to develop, since this will give the candidate the chance to react spontaneously and to depend less on the teacher's input. However, it is important that if the candidate 'dries up' the teacher is ready with another question to carry the conversation on. In almost all speaking tests there are some uncomfortable silences: the teacher should not be responsible for these!

Follow up closed questions, such as those which prompt Yes/No or one-word answers, with a request for further information whenever possible. (See suggestions later in this chapter, and also in Chapter 5.)

Ask questions which are as open as possible, since they give candidates more chance to shine than closed ones (which prompt, for example, a list). Better candidates benefit from being asked at least some very open questions, such as 'Tell me about ...'/ 'Describe ...'.

Give candidates the opportunity to refer to past, present and future, and express opinions. It is best not to leave this too late in the test. Candidates may benefit from a couple of fairly undemanding opening questions to put them at their ease, but for many candidates the teacher has to provide a number of opportunities for reference to the past or (especially) the future, before one of them is successful. Since without these references candidates **cannot** meet the Grade C requirements, there must be enough time to try again (and again and again!).

Ask questions which give the best candidates a chance to give reasons, and to justify their ideas ('What do you think of …?/Why?' 'Explain …')

Take into account the ability of the candidate when applying the above. There is no point in pursuing a future reference with a Grade F candidate – it would be much better to spend the time making sure that he or she communicates at least a few basic facts, and perhaps a simple opinion, clearly.

Listen to the answers given by candidates! Especially towards the end of a long session, it is easy for the teacher to go onto 'auto-pilot'. This is important because the candidate will get no credit for repeating the same information. Even more crucially, if the teacher asks the candidate 'What does your brother do for a living?', and then repeats the question 30 seconds later, the candidate may panic, thinking that he or she made an error the first time. This can seriously affect the rest of the candidate's performance.

Try to indicate clearly a change of topic (*Ahora discutiremos …*). Many candidates fail to understand properly the first question on a new subject because they are expecting another question on the previous topic.

Avoid repeating, or even worse, correcting, the candidate's answers.

Allow the **candidate** to speak as much as possible. Within the requirement that the conversation must be a dialogue, and not a monologue by the candidate, the less the teacher says the better.

Candidates might find it useful to have a copy of the following suggestions during their preparations for the Speaking test.

Suggestions for candidates

ROLE PLAYS

Foundation Tier

- Only prepare what you need to say.

- Remember the English instructions are not for translation, they are to tell you what to say. If it says *Ask your friend if he/she likes football* it means *Say: 'Do you like football?'*

- If you have a choice, make sure you choose an item you know in the foreign language.

Foundation/Higher and Higher Tier

- It's worth giving a bit of thought to the unprepared bit (when you have a **!** on your card, or are told to answer the question). You may be able to work out what sort of question the teacher is likely to ask.

- If you have to **ask** a question, think particularly carefully about how to do it. Lots of candidates make a mess of asking questions.

(With acknowledgments to Geoff Shooter, Principal Examiner, Speaking, AQA GCSE French)

P © CILT 2003

PRESENTATION

- Practise **out loud**.

- **Time** your Presentation.

- **Record** it on cassette.

- Make sure your notes/cue cards give you what **you** need.

- Include **past**, **present**, and **future**, and some **opinions**. You could use a checklist like the one for the Writing test.

- **Don't rush** or gabble.

- **Listen** to the teacher's questions for the discussion.

GENERAL CONVERSATION

- Have some ready-made phrases for each topic. They come in handy for when you get stuck, and they provide useful extra details.

- Go further than a bare minimum answer whenever you can, for example in answer to the question: *Tu as des frères ou des sœurs? J'ai un frère qui s'appelle John* is better than just *J'ai un frère*, and adding *Il a treize ans* is even better.

- Try not to leave too long gaps. Say you don't understand so your teacher can move on.

GOING BEYOND THE MINIMUM

The following examples show how an adequate series of questions and answers can be run together to form a much higher level response, without requiring a great deal more in terms of structures, and in the first example with almost no extra vocabulary. You should aim to give at least some B-type answers in your Speaking test.

A

Q *Erzähle mir ein wenig von deiner Familie.*
A Ich habe einen Bruder und eine Schwester.

Q *Wie heißen sie?*
A Mein Bruder heißt Peter und meine Schwester heißt Zoë.

Q *Wie alt sind sie?*
A Mein Bruder ist fünfzehn und meine Schwester ist dreizehn Jahre alt.

Q *Verstehst du dich gut mit ihnen?*
A Ich verstehe mich gut mit Peter und Zoë.

Q *¿Qué tipo de música te gusta?*
A Me gusta la música rock.

Q *¿Porqué?*
A Porque hace mucho ruido.

Q *¿Cuál es tu grupo preferido?*
A Me gusta sobre todo Iron Maiden.

Q *¿Sabes tocar un instrumento?*
Q Si, toco el violín.

B

Q *Erzähle mir ein wenig von deiner Familie.*
A Ich habe einen Bruder, der Peter heißt, und eine Schwester, die Zoë heißt. Peter ist fünfzehn Jahre alt und Zoë ist dreizehn. Ich verstehe mich gut mit ihnen.

Q *¿Qué tipo de música te gusta?*
A Me gusta la música rock, porque hace mucho ruido. Creo que el mejor grupo es Iron Maiden. Pero me gusta también la música clásica. Toco el violín en una orquesta de mi pueblo y hago ejercicios todos los jueves por la tarde.

Speaking criteria (Key elements in the criteria for assessment of Speaking at GCSE)

GRADE ▼	Communication/ Content	Quality/Application of Language	Accuracy
A	• Spontaneous interchange • Understands questions • Takes initiative • Beyond minimum • Ideas • Justifies points of view • Descriptions	• Range of structures and vocabulary • Longer sequences • Pronunciation and intonation very accurate • Variety of tenses	• Generally accurate • Few major errors • Errors do not affect meaning
C	• Main points communicated • Some additional details • Simple personal opinions	• (Limited) range of structures and vocabulary • Basic style • Occasional English influence • Sentences repetitive • Attempts at tenses • Pronunciation generally accurate • Some hesitation	• More accurate than inaccurate • Messages clear
F	• Laboured – examiner does most of work • Simple questions, often rephrased • Some points communicated	• Very limited vocabulary • Pronunciation approximate • Few structures • Pre-learnt phrases	• Brief, often monosyllabic • Few correct verbs

key points	• Thorough preparation by the teacher and realistic practice by the candidate can help reduce the stress of the test.
	• Students need lots of practice in asking questions in the target language.
	• The pre-prepared element should be a good confidence-booster for the Conversation.
	• Good students must always be looking for ways to go beyond the minimum – encouraged by appropriate teacher questions.

Writing

chapter 5

☐ How can Grade F/G students communicate in writing?
  - at the level of individual words?
  - in sentences?

☐ How can Grade D students improve their writing to Grade C?
  - in sentences?
  - in paragraphs?

☐ How can Grade A students make sure they achieve their potential in writing?
  - in paragraphs?
  - throughout a whole piece?

☐ Why choose the Coursework option?

☐ How much help can students be given with coursework?

How can Grade F/G students communicate in writing?

As in speaking, students who operate at the lowest level do not often generate their own sentences in the foreign language.

The first question(s) in the Foundation Tier Writing test will usually simply require candidates to list items of vocabulary. They need to have practice in this kind of exercise – writing a shopping list or a list of items to take on a picnic, for example – so that they build up a bank of concrete nouns which they can spell sufficiently accurately to be recognisable, within the more likely topics in the Specification. A good score in this question will put a candidate very close to the ten Uniform Marks which equate in any skill to a Grade G performance. Some awarding bodies may specify a group of items (for example, by giving pictures), from which the candidate must select his or her answer, while others may simply give the type of item needed, leaving the candidate to produce the necessary number of items. Especially in the former case, students need constant reminders to choose items which they are confident they know. It is perhaps worth mentioning at this point, especially since this level of student often relies disproportionately on cognates or near cognates, that an error in spelling which produces an English word (geography for *géographie,* for example) will normally be given no credit.

The next question(s) will demand the production of a short message. While responses in sentences may be required to score high marks in this question, **some** marks may be available for brief answers, sometimes single words or short phrases. Students should be trained to read the rubric carefully to see what is needed, to come up with the minimalist answer, which they can then try to put into a sentence.

If the task is to say what they do on Saturday, tell them:

- first of all to write down an appropriate activity: *les courses;*
- then try to put in a suitable verb: *Je fais.*

Even if they can't come up with the verb, the activity alone may be enough to get some credit.

The final question on the Foundation Tier Writing test will require candidates to write continuously in the target language – usually in the form of a letter – and may require candidates to complete certain specified tasks, or to respond to a stimulus letter/e-mail in the target language. Students at this level should again be encouraged to read the rubric, which will be in English, carefully, and to write down any sentences they can remember which are relevant to the set tasks. Even a bank of half a dozen pre-learnt sentences on each of the topics in the Specification can be sufficient to enable candidates to complete at least part of this question.

If they are to have any chance of credit in this question, students must be trained **not** to respond to the tasks in English, and then translate their answers into the target language, but to rely on what they **remember** from their language lessons. It must be said that the least able students often produce little which is worthy of credit in this question, and this may be one reason for considering entering them for Coursework (see later section), which may give them a better chance of showing what they can do.

While the 'minimalist' approach suggested above should not be taken as a recipe for teaching low-ability students from Year 7 – clearly these students need to be encouraged to produce 'joined-up' French/German/Spanish to make their study of a language worthwhile – there is every reason for concentrating, during the run-up to the exam, on those elements of the test in which they are likely to have some success.

How can Grade D students improve their writing to Grade C?

For these students, encouragement to maximise their success in the shorter answers as suggested above is still important, though they will rely less on pre-learnt material, since they will have internalised much more in the way of vocabulary and simple sentence structure.

In the longer answers, there are a number of crucial elements:

Tasks

- The question set will include a number of required tasks. These may be specifically identified – by bullet points or numbers – or may be incorporated in the body of the question. However these tasks are presented, it is **essential** that they are covered in the answer.
- The marks for Communication/Content will in part depend on the proportion of the tasks completed; a totally accurate answer which only responds to half of the tasks will probably be eligible for no more than half of the marks for Communication/Content.
- In some cases (e.g. AQA), the mark for Content will put a ceiling on the marks for Quality of Language and Accuracy.

Choice of questions

- Students need to be trained to make any choice of question work for them. In order to make a sensible choice, they should:
  - a) have an idea of which are their best (and weakest) topic areas, so that they can, for example, quickly reject a question which strongly features an area for which they have little vocabulary;
  - b) very quickly read through the tasks to identify any which require vocabulary they don't know/have forgotten. Though the tasks (particularly at overlap) may not be very vocabulary specific, they will all require some vocabulary within the relevant area.
- If students are to have enough time:
  - a) to complete all the tasks;
  - b) to check their answers for range and accuracy;

  they need practice in making their choice **quickly**. Students of limited ability in particular will probably spend relatively longer on the early, shorter questions, and will not therefore have time to spare for protracted agonising over their choice. If the relevant awarding body offers options (Edexcel and OCR), at least some of the writing tasks students are asked to do, particularly in class, should feature some element of choice.

Quality of Language

- The Grade Description for Grade C in writing requires candidates to 'express personal opinions' and to include reference to 'past, present and future events [and] involving the use of different tenses.'
- The assessment criteria for this level also refer to variety or range of structures and vocabulary.
- It may be helpful to encourage in students the habit of using a checklist such as the one at the end of this section whenever they produce a piece of written work. This is not intended for the teacher to use – though in giving feedback to students it will certainly be useful for pointing out ways of improvement – but for the students to apply independently. This will give them a regular reminder of the 'hoops' which they are required to jump through in order to achieve their potential mark, and they should aim to tick as many of possible of the asterisked points in every piece of work, and more than one example of the items marked ** in the checklist below.
- Even if the assessment criteria allow candidates to achieve a particular mark with just one example each of (for example) a past tense, a future tense and a personal opinion, students should be encouraged to attempt more than one in each case. For if the one attempt at, say, a past does not work, this will certainly mean that the appropriate point on the assessment criteria **cannot** be achieved.

Accuracy

- This is more a measure of how much language has been internalised by the student over a period of time than a matter of good exam technique, but a mechanical checklist such as the one which follows may help him or her to spend a useful final two or three minutes ensuring that there are no avoidable errors in an answer.
- Since at this level a key measure of inaccuracy is how far it impedes communication, it may help borderline students to concentrate on the essential element of a task, and to ensure that this is carried out as accurately as possible, before checking the extra details and developments.
- The regular use of a checklist, such as the one shown on the next page, when completing class- or homework, will encourage students to mentally check their answers in the exam itself.

French checklist Grade C

In this piece of work I have: **Tick** or number used

- completed all the tasks; ☐
- included details beyond those required by the task; ☐
- **included some personal opinions; ☐
- *linked ideas (*et; mais; puis; donc*); ☐
- **referred to the present; ☐
- **referred to the past (*J'ai/Je suis ...é*); ☐
- **referred to the future (*Je vais ...er*); ☐
- *used an adverb (*rapidement*); ☐
- *used adjectives; ☐
- *given a reason (*parce que ...*); ☐
- *used a qui clause (*J'ai un frère qui s'appelle ...*); ☐

I have also checked that:

- if I mean present, I have used the verb with the right ending (not ending in -*é*, and not using *je suis*); ☐
- if I mean perfect, I have used *j'ai* or *je suis* with the past participle (often ending -*é*); ☐
- as far as I know, genders (*le/la/un/une*) are correct; ☐
- as far as I know, accents are correct; ☐
- adjectives agree with feminine/plural nouns. ☐

Note: This checklist can in no circumstances be used **by the teacher** to replace or supplement the approved coursework Comments Sheet, which is **the only way** in which the teacher can give feedback on a first draft. The suggested checklist may be used **independently** by the student to check his or her own work.

P © CILT 2003

How can Grade A students make sure they achieve their potential in writing?

As is the case at every level, students at the highest level need to make sure that they first of all fulfil the lesser requirements mentioned above. Good students need to demonstrate their ability to use as much as possible of the grammar and structures section of the Specification, and to do so with some confidence – which in the case of the basic requirements (such as justifying opinions and referring to past, present and future) means doing it **more than once**. Students at this level should therefore be encouraged to include, particularly in the Higher Tier question, as many as possible of the asterisked points in the checklist on p50, including several examples of the items marked **.

The best students should aim to consciously avoid repetition, by using synonyms, pronouns and alternative structures. For example, when describing holiday activities, they should be taught to write *Lundi, j'ai joué au tennis avec ma sœur, et puis mardi on a fait une partie de boules* rather than *Lundi, j'ai joué au tennis avec ma sœur, et puis mardi j'ai joué aux boules*.

These students, perhaps more than any others, need to know in detail how the criteria for assessment work. Their knowledge and application of the language are by definition very good, but unless they know the importance of including a range of different structures, including tenses, they may produce what is to them a perfectly good response which fails to score the very highest marks (see Chapter 8).

Planning a piece of work is also crucial to attain the maximum score. Although the detailed tasks within a question will inevitably form the basis of the plan, it can be helpful to note also the structures to be included within each task, as in the following example.

Higher level task

Some Spanish visitors are coming to spend a fortnight in the area where you live. You have been asked to send them some information to help them plan their visit.

Escribe tus ideas y opiniones sobre todos los temas siguientes explicando por qué piensas así:
- *el tiempo que hace:*
- *atracciones turísticas;*
- *la vida nocturna;*
- *una ciudad local que vale la pena visitar.*

*Escribe en **español** sobre **todos** los temas indicados.*

PLAN

1 Often cold. Hope it will be fine. But bring jumper and raincoat. If rains can go shopping in town, then eat a pizza.

2 Description of castle. When it was built and who used to live there. Oldest in England. Very interesting because can visit kitchen. Can also go to lake. Would be super because lots to do.

3 At night will go to leisure centre. I went last week – great time with friends – played football. Also good film at cinema if you've not seen it.

4 Must go to York. Old walled city. I went last year. Had never been before. Good museum where you ride on a train – less tiring than walking. When we've visited museum we will buy some local chocolates.

This could of course be done in the target language, but may take longer. The above plan in English should only take a few minutes, and gives opportunities to include:

1	2	3	4
• Present, future, imperative, infinitive. • Subordinate clauses, linking of ideas.	• Description using present, past, adjectives, subordinate clause. • Opinions and justifications. • Superlative. • Conditional.	• Future, past, present. • Subordinate clause. • Change of person. • Negative.	• Description. • Past, pluperfect, future, perfect infinitive. • Different negative. • Subordinate clause. • Comparison.

French checklist Grade A

In this piece of work I have:　　　　　　　　　　**Tick** or number used

- completed **all** the tasks; ☐
- included details beyond those required by the task using **complete sentences;** ☐
- *included some personal opinions; ☐
- *linked ideas (*et; mais; puis; donc*); ☐
- **given reasons (*parce que ...*) for some opinions; ☐
- **referred to the **present;** ☐
- **referred to the past (*J'ai/Je suis ...é*); ☐
- **referred to the **future;** ☐
- *used a **future** (*Je ...erai/irai*); ☐
- *used an **imperfect** (*Je ...ais*); ☐
- *used a **pluperfect** (*J'avais ...é*); ☐
- *used a **conditional** (*Je ...erais/irais*); ☐
- *used an **adverb** (*rapidement*); ☐
- *used **adjectives;** ☐
- *used a *qui* clause (*J'ai un frère **qui** s'appelle ...*); ☐
- *used a *que (qu')* clause (*... l'émission **que** j'ai vue ...*); ☐
- *used *depuis;* ☐
- *used *après avoir;* ☐
- *made a **comparison** (*plus ... que/moins ... que*); ☐

I have also checked that:

- if I mean **present,** I have used the verb with the right ending; ☐
- if I mean **perfect,** I have used *avoir* or *être* + past participle; ☐
- as far as I know, genders (*le/la/un/une*) are correct; ☐
- as far as I know, accents are correct; ☐
- adjectives agree with feminine/plural nouns. ☐

Note: This checklist can in no circumstances be used **by the teacher** to replace or supplement the approved coursework Comments Sheet, which is **the only way** in which the teacher can give feedback on a first draft. The suggested checklist may be used **independently** by the student to check his or her own work. **P** © CILT 2003

Going beyond the minimum

In an essay on healthy lifestyles, here are some ideas for expanding on basic notions. Similar ideas for German and Spanish are shown in the appendix.

Je suis en forme.

➡ **Je pense que** *je suis* **assez** *en forme* **en ce moment.**

Je mangeais trop de bonbons. Je mangeais souvent dans les restaurants fast-food.

➡ **Quand j'étais plus jeune,** *je* **mangeais** *beaucoup de* **choses sucrées, comme** *les bonbons et le chocolat.* **En plus** *j'allais souvent aux restaurants fast-food* **avec mes copains, alors** *j'étais un peu gros, et je n'étais* **pas du tout** *en forme.*

Maintenant je mange des fruits et des légumes.

➡ *Maintenant,* **j'ai changé** *de régime, et j'essaie* **de manger** *des fruits et des légumes, et* **de ne pas** *grignoter. Je* **ne** *vais* **plus** *beaucoup chez McDo.*

Je suis très sportive. Je fais partie de l'équipe de football du collège. On a un match tous les samedis.

➡ **J'ai toujours été** *assez sportive, car j'adore le foot et la natation.* **Maintenant que** *je fais partie de l'équipe de football du collège,* **qui** *a beaucoup de réussite* **en ce moment,** *je m'entraîne* **trois fois par semaine,** *et on a un match presque* **tous les samedis,** *alors pour l'exercice ça va.*

Je fume des cigarettes. Je veux être comme mes amis. Ce n'est pas bon pour la santé.

➡ *Malheureusement, l'année dernière j'ai commencé* **à fumer.** *J'ai fait ça* **pour être** *comme mes amis, mais je sais bien* **que** *c'est stupide. La dernière fois* **que** *j'ai joué au foot, je n'ai pas pu courir.*

Je ne vais pas fumer. Je vais me coucher à onze heures.

➡ *J'ai* **donc** *décidé de renoncer aux cigarettes tout de suite. Je vais aussi me coucher* **avant** *onze heures pendant la semaine,* **parce que** *je suis souvent fatigué en classe, et c'est bientôt les examens. Alors, je* **serai** *très en forme, n'est-ce pas?*

Why choose the Coursework option?

Weak students may benefit from:

- less demand on memory – they can check grammar notes, etc while they are producing their assignment (except in controlled conditions);
- teacher comments on a first draft;
- support from the teacher, which may result in a sense of achievement, rather than the sense of failure such students inevitably feel in the Writing test (where most of the tasks are beyond their ability);
- the possibility of choosing their best assignments from a number of attempts;
- rapid feedback on assignments, and immediate awareness of progress towards the target grade.

Able students may benefit from many of the above, plus:

- the possibility of selecting a title which is of interest;
- topics which may lead more naturally to further study (e.g. AS level);
- time after the completion of coursework during which they can concentrate on the other three skills.

Teachers may in addition benefit from parity with other subjects, whose coursework demands can interfere with students' ability or willingness to produce written MFL homework which 'doesn't count' towards their final grade. Many teachers have pointed out that, if the Coursework option is to be chosen, it can be helpful to begin a 'coursework approach' to written work during Key Stage 3, by giving students the opportunity to produce a first draft of extended pieces of writing which they can refine after the teacher's comments.

For an overview of the whole issue of coursework in GCSE foreign languages, see Pathfinder 35: *On course for GCSE coursework* (Adams 2002).

It is important to note that the following general advice should be considered in the light of the Coursework regulations and requirements in each Specification.

How much help can students be given with coursework?

In answering this question, the most important thing to remember is that in any piece of coursework, it is only the **student's** contribution which is assessed. While it might be appropriate to give weaker students a great deal of help, including at the lowest level some form of template on which to base their response, the degree of help given will be reflected in the assessment. An assignment in which the student simply supplies missing words or phrases in a questionnaire, for example, will only qualify for Grade G, since Grade F requires that candidates 'write short sentences' in addition to responding to written texts by 'substituting words and set phrases' (see Grade Descriptions).

It therefore follows that it is not in the interests of students to give them a degree of help which would limit their possible mark unnecessarily. If a profile of a Spanish pop singer is used to stimulate the production of a profile of Britney Spears, a good candidate must realise that an identical profile, simply changing details of age, family and discs released will result in quite low marks, and that what is required is the student's own language. This can be quite a tricky message to get across, and it may be that for many students this kind of approach is not suitable.

On the other hand, at GCSE level, students generally only give back the language which the teacher has given them, whether in an exam or in coursework, and there is no reason that the nature of the teaching should be significantly different whether students are entered for Coursework or for the terminal exam. They still need to be given examples of linguistic structures in use, patterns of language such as verb paradigms and to practise sentence construction. At this stage, the fact that they will be able to refer to their exercise books when producing their Coursework assignments (with the exception of the final version of the controlled conditions assignment) is irrelevant.

Once the teacher has set the assignment, he or she should have no further direct input into the language the students use, other than through the **Comments Sheet** to be used for the first draft. It must be said that the Comments Sheet is not very user-friendly, and should probably only be used 'cold' with the very best students.

Although the sheet itself **may not be adapted in any way,** some advance planning can make it more helpful.

Preparing students to use the Coursework Comments Sheet

- Before setting any Coursework assignments, explain clearly what a tick in each box would mean. (See example on next page.) This could be expanded, possibly by using an exploded version for classroom display.
- Be as precise as possible, and for weaker students leave as few alternatives as possible. For example, 'Give more opinions = Use *j'aime* or *je n'aime pas*'.
- For very weak students, it may be most helpful to use only a few of the boxes (e.g. those marked with an asterisk on the example), and to simplify even more, for example, 'Check spellings and accents = Only end a word in *é* after *j'ai* or *je suis*', even at the risk of over-simplifying.

For a very weak group, ask yourself if the use of a draft with its accompanying Comments Sheet is likely to result in a **better** final version. If the answer is 'Probably not', consider not asking for a first draft. Consider also the possibility that the draft may be as good as, or better than, the final version. It is quite within the rules to submit the draft as the final version, as long as the student has not had the opportunity to amend it.

CONTENT

TASK COMPLETION

Some parts of the task have not been covered	**You have not mentioned one of the bullet points.**
Fails to meet the requirements of the task	**Much of what you have written is not relevant to the title.**

PRESENTATION

*Presentation and layout to be tidied up	**Use a separate paragraph for each bullet point AND/OR Write more neatly.**

INTEREST

Add some more ideas/introduction/ conclusion	**Include first paragraph saying what the assignment is about AND/OR Include last paragraph pulling together what you have written, and saying what you think about it AND/OR Give more details about events OR Add more events.**
Give more description	**Add some adjectives AND/OR describing sentences. – *C'était [un grand bâtiment rouge].***
*Give more opinions/reasons	**Use *j'aime/je n'aime pas/je pense que* AND/OR Add *parce que/car/à cause de.***
Vary type of sentence more	**Use linking words to make longer sentences AND/OR Use *qui/que/quand/où.***
*Vary your vocabulary more	**If you have used the same word more than once, try to find a different word, e.g. *C'était super/C'était formidable/C'était passionnant.***

QUALITY OF LANGUAGE

*Check spellings and accents	**Use your dictionary if you are not sure AND/OR Make sure past participles of ...*er* verbs end in *é*.**
Check verb tenses and formation	**Check verb endings [never *je* followed by ...*es* or ...*t*/never *il/elle* followed by ...*s*] AND/OR Make sure past tenses have part of *avoir/être* + past participle AND/OR Make sure you have referred to PAST and PRESENT and FUTURE.**
Check word order	**Check adverbs (e.g. *souvent*) come after verb.**
Check nouns and genders	**Use your dictionary if you are not sure.**
Check adjectives and agreements	**Adjectives after *la/les* will (usually) end ...*e*/...*s*.**

Feedback is a crucial part of Coursework. Although the only feedback allowed on a 'live' assignment is through the Coursework Comments Sheet, it is good practice to give students a detailed analysis of the strengths and weaknesses of a completed assignment so that they can improve their performance in future pieces. Clearly, this can only be done once the final version is in the hands of the teacher. It may therefore be useful to mark a photocopy of the piece, which can then be discussed with the student.

Teachers may also find it useful, possibly at the beginning of Year 10, to get students to do a 'dummy' assignment, so that some of the requirements for producing a good piece of coursework can be discussed in concrete terms, and the use of the Comments Sheet can be demonstrated.

key points	• **Students who have problems with long-term memory and long-term goals will benefit from the Coursework option.** • **However, this option should not be ignored for the best students.** • **Both in Coursework and in the Writing test, answering the question is vital.** • **Planning and writing must take into account the criteria for assessment if students are to achieve their potential.** • **Except at the most basic level, some instances of developing basic statements are needed to gain higher marks.**

Listening

☐ A skill to be taught, rather than just tested!

☐ How can students be encouraged to practise listening?

☐ How important is the equipment used?

☐ What techniques do students need in order to succeed in the Listening test?

chapter 6

A skill to be taught, rather than just tested!

Listening is a neglected skill, not because we don't do enough of it, but because we too often treat it simply as a way of testing or practising the grammar and structures we have taught, rather than as a skill in its own right – a skill which our students may not have acquired very well even in their own language.

Just because the GCSE exam uses only authentic target language spoken by native speakers and recorded on cassette, there is no reason for language lessons to limit themselves to this. If their listening consists exclusively of the recorded items included in the coursebook, supplemented in Years 10 and 11 by past GCSE listening tests, students will see listening as a means of testing their comprehension of newly-learnt vocabulary and structures. This is clearly a necessary part of training for GCSE, but unless students are aware of **how** to listen effectively, it is a skill they are unlikely to perform well.

It is possible to practise listening skills. By this is meant not acquiring the techniques required in the Listening test, which will be referred to later, but practising:

- word separation;
- liaison;
- elision;
- sound patterns (see *Strategies*).

A five-minute, teacher-read exercise where the object is to pick out where one word ends and the next begins (a sort of dictation without the spelling) can be a good exercise to practise the vital ability to separate what is heard into words. Equally valid (though not in the least authentic) are exercises practising recognising numbers **in context**. This is particularly important in French, where liaison can often mean that the number heard is significantly different from the number learnt: *deux heures* sounds quite different from the number *deu(x)* chanted by the student in Year 7. Also in French, it is often only the vowel sound which distinguishes two quite different numbers (*deux enfants* from *douze enfants, trois hommes* from *treize hommes,* etc).

However, large numbers are also difficult in all languages, because the mode of acquisition is often via the written figure, and it is only at a very high level that this goes into the learner's mind in the target language. For most English readers the date 2003 will be read in English ('two thousand and three') even in the middle of a French/German/Spanish sentence. The **sound** of the number is therefore rarely met except by deliberate intent.

Listening discrimination exercises from an early age can pay dividends:

bois – bois – mois – bois

Pick the odd one out. NB it's not just vowels that are hard – *b/p, m/n, d/t, f/v* are difficult too. Negatives are crucial – missing them turns the whole meaning upside down. It is worth practising (again perhaps by odd-one-out exercises) picking them out in a variety of sentences.

Even before candidates begin listening for meaning, they can try to work out exactly what they are listening **for**. It is worth getting students to look at some questions just in order to work out what sort of information is required.

- Identifying specific details – this often relies on recognising individual items of vocabulary. It is often possible to work out from the question whether a number, a colour, an activity, a place, etc is needed even **before** listening to the target language.
- Identifying opinions – again, a question such as 'What does X think about …?' could mean that phrases such as 'I like/don't like' will be key to the answer.
- On the other hand, beyond Grade C, students should be aware that the answer is more likely to depend on understanding the overall message. They should therefore **only** pick out an isolated word as their answer if they really haven't understood the whole thing. Typical questions to test gist comprehension might be: 'What is X's **attitude** to …?' or 'How does X **react** to …?'

At a higher level, candidates will often be expected to spot the link between a word in the question and a **synonym** on the cassette. This can again be practised through teacher-delivered sentences where the student is given a list of four words, and asked to pick out the one which is a (near) synonym for the key word in the spoken sentence. Also at a higher level, students may need the ability to draw conclusions from indicators such as conjunctions or prepositions (*aber, vor, nach*), use of tenses, expressions of agreement or disagreement. Like the above, practice in this skill can be more focused if the teacher simply reads out sentences containing the relevant structures.

Listening comprehension requires before all else a knowledge of the vocabulary heard. The lowest level Foundation questions will deliberately target single words: the student hears a number of people saying what their favourite leisure activity is, and for each speaker the candidate has to choose the correct picture of a leisure activity. However, candidates will frequently score a mark, even on a Grade C item, simply for picking out the key word: the student hears two people discussing their weekend, and has to fill in a grid showing what they did when. It may be necessary to put two ideas together (Saturday night and cinema) but the emphasis is still on vocabulary. Even at the highest level, where students are required to understand more complex ideas involving grammatical structures, one of the most common reasons for failure to gain the mark is a gap in vocabulary. (For ideas on vocabulary learning, see Chapter 1.)

At the very highest level, students are expected to draw conclusions from what they hear. This means that, while at a lower level, they might be expected to understand that someone is happy because they use the word 'happy' or 'pleased', at around Grade A, they need to work out that someone is happy **without** their using the actual word: 'I get good marks, I have a lot of friends and my teachers are nice' leads to the conclusion that the speaker is happy at school.

Just as in reading (see Chapter 7) there are different kinds of texts, so in listening there are different kinds of recordings, which may require slightly different approaches:

- **Short monologues.** These may be single-sentence utterances, often tested through multiple-choice questions (often relying on a key word or words);
- **Longer monologues.** These may in fact be 'interview' situations, where a short question is followed by a longer response. The question will indicate whether gist or detailed comprehension is required;
- **Dialogues.** These can be more tricky, in that it can be important who says what. The recording will always stress a change of speaker, possibly by somewhat unnatural use of names, and may well alternate different voices (e.g. male/female).

The question will often make clear if it is important to distinguish between speakers, for example 'What does X think about ...?' 'And what does Y think?'
- **Conversations.** Again, the recording will use names to show who is speaking. Questions which give (in the target language) a series of statements, and ask the candidate to match each statement to the appropriate person, are often used here.

How can students be encouraged to practise listening?

In one sense, students get more practice in listening than in any other skill, since in every lesson they hear the teacher speaking in the target language. However, this can in itself be a very **testing** experience, and students are adept at avoiding the demands it makes, either through laziness, or so as not to be made to look silly. How many students, when the teacher gives a simple target language instruction such as 'Turn to page 57', look at their neighbour to see what he or she does, or look embarrassed when the teacher finds they are on the wrong page? There is no doubt that the more students hear of the target language in the classroom, the easier – because the more familiar – listening becomes, but it may be helpful to take some of the pressure off students in this particularly demanding skill.

Simple conversations between two students, which they have prepared for speaking practice, can easily be used for listening for gist (Where are they? What has just happened? What happens next?).

In many ways, it is better if recorded material is somewhat below the students' level of ability, as this will add to their confidence in listening. This can be a particular problem with the cassettes used with coursebooks, as they are often designed to practise and test the most recently taught structures, and are therefore at the top of students' linguistic ability, and contain the least well known vocabulary and grammar. Some practice using the same topic from the previous year's coursebook, or, if the coursebook is divided into different books for different abilities, from the lower level book, can boost students' confidence in their ability to listen.

If students can be given cassettes to take home, it can make a big difference. They can listen at their own pace, replaying several times if necessary, until they are satisfied they've understood. Providing listening cassettes to take home need not be a burden on the budget. It may be possible, for example, to record small sections from the cassette which accompanies the coursebook onto students' own cassettes for them to practise listening at home. Equally, the Foreign Language Assistant could be asked to record exercises such as those described in the first section of this chapter. Such home listening may well focus, not on the comprehension-testing aspect of listening, but on developing the **habit** and **skills** of listening.

Listening at home is also partly a question of student perception – if listening is something we only do as a whole class, it's not as important (and it's probably more boring) than the other skills. Including listening activities as part of group work can also improve the status of listening, as well as giving students a less challenging atmosphere than whole-class work.

Transcripts can be used very successfully to bridge the gap between students' comprehension of the written word and their understanding of the spoken word. Used **before** listening, they help students to concentrate on matching the sounds they hear with the words they see, and make easier the difficulty of identifying where one word ends and the next begins. This works wonders for students' sense of achievement. Used **after** a listening comprehension exercise they will help to ensure that students learn something from the listening experience. A gapped transcript used **during** listening can focus on new vocabulary or grammar.

How important is the equipment used?

The importance of the quality and maintenance of sound equipment, and its availability at the right time in the right place, cannot be over-emphasised. Since the widespread use of tapes/cassettes in the language classroom began in the 1960s, how many thousands of students have rapidly been convinced that they could not 'do listening' simply because they couldn't cope with the 'fuzz' issuing from the department's one tape player with its inadequate speaker?

In the classroom

- The quality of reproduction depends mainly on the speaker(s) used. Obviously, in most classrooms, connecting the cassette player to external speakers is not possible (but see later remarks about the equipment used in exams). Suppliers of audio equipment offer a range of cassette players: it is important to choose machines which are recommended for full classroom use if they are to depend on the internal speaker.
- In the interests of economy, it is worth considering whether all the machines need to have a recording capability, as this will probably be used much less frequently than playback.
- A kit which allows a number of headsets to be used with a single cassette player is very useful if group work is envisaged. Listening quality is usually enhanced by using headsets.
- If the equipment is to be used by a number of teachers, or is to be carried from classroom to classroom, robustness is a consideration. If it is possible to allocate a machine for use by each teacher, this can help reduce wear and tear, as well as ensuring that cassettes can be used whenever appropriate, without the need to plan equipment in advance. The same is truc if it is possible to have a cassette player available in each room where languages are taught.
- The quality of the room can also play a part in success in listening, especially perhaps in older buildings with high ceilings. Reports by OFSTED inspectors have been known to win funds for false ceilings or carpets in MFL classrooms!

In the examination

There are two factors to consider, which are mutually dependent:

- **The room** which is normally used for external exams may be very large – the school hall or the sports hall, for example. Before its use is agreed for the Listening test, it is essential that the availability of **suitable** equipment is established. In any room seating more than twenty or so candidates at regulation distance one from another, it will almost always be necessary to use external speakers to achieve adequate sound quality. Check sound quality in **different parts** of a large room – the difference is often considerable. In a very large space, even this may not be enough, since sports halls in particular are often high, with many hard surfaces. In such cases, it is better to split the candidates into a number of smaller rooms. If rooms are available with carpets and curtains, so much the better. Clearly, in real schools, the ideal is rarely available, and some compromise will be inevitable, but it is important to remember that sound quality can make an enormous difference to the performance of students, and to try to achieve the best possible conditions.

- **The equipment** should in many ways determine the rooms used, despite the added administrative problems caused by using a number of rooms – it may be necessary to find alternative rooms for other classes, and to provide staff to control noise in corridors, etc.

What techniques do students need in order to succeed in the Listening test?

A checklist such as the one shown opposite could be given to students at the start of their GCSE course or they could be given the specific points as the teacher feels appropriate.

key points	• Listening doesn't have to be pre-recorded material used to test comprehension or acquisition of newly-learnt vocabulary and structures. It can equally be material read out by the teacher, which is relevant to the topic being covered, but which uses mainly familiar vocabulary and structures, in order to increase students' self-confidence in listening. • Students need to learn how to listen, developing other skills than just comprehension. • There are different kinds of listening for comprehension, which require different approaches. • Buy the best sound equipment you can afford.

Advice for students

BEFORE EACH ITEM

Read the rubric/question carefully. Work out what sort of information you are listening for (a number/colour/place/attitude). If there are pictures, try to remember the target language for the picture, so you'll recognise it when you hear it.

Look at the mark allocation – usually if there's more than one mark, you need more than one piece of information.

WHEN THE TAPE IS PLAYING

Listen. If you get the answer after the first listening, that's fine. If you are in any doubt, make notes if you like – of words/phrases you recognise – but don't be distracted from **listening.** In the pause, write your answer, or any ideas you have. Then **listen** again to the second playing – don't write anything until the tape has stopped, then either confirm or change your answer.

EXAM TECHNIQUES

(Equally appropriate for the Reading test)

- **Answers** can be one word or phrase at Foundation Tier, but sometimes need more.

- **Answers** must be legible. (But if you want to make rough notes, do so – neatness in that sense doesn't matter).

- Make sure you answer questions in the right way – a letter (A, B, C etc), a name, a tick – and in the **correct language.** If you need to answer in words, the language of your answer should be the same as the language of the question. It is not uncommon at Higher in the harder, English questions, for candidates to answer in French/German/Spanish, but an answer in the wrong language will gain **no marks,** even if it gives the correct information.

- If you need to change an answer, particularly a multiple-choice answer, **cross out** your original answer, and write in the new one next to it. Never try to change a **B** to make it into a **D** – the chances are the examiner won't be able to tell which letter you meant, and so won't give you the mark.

- Look at the example, if there is one. It will give you an idea of much you need to write. If the answer in the example is a single word in the target language, then a single word is enough to score the mark.

- Look at the mark allocation for the question. A mark of 2 will usually indicate that two pieces of information are required.

- Don't leave answers blank if you can help it – and never in multiple-choice questions.

- Use your knowledge of life in the target language country. For example, if you hear the price of something, but don't quite catch it, try to think of likely prices. An ice-cream is more likely to cost €1.50 (about £1) than €15 (about £10).

Reading

chapter 7

☐ A skill to be taught, rather than just tested!

☐ What makes students want to read in the target language (TL)?

☐ How can students cope with unknown words?

☐ What techniques are needed for success in the Reading test?

A skill to be taught, rather than just tested!

Teaching reading skills is obviously a huge issue. (For an overview, see Pathfinder 36: *More reading for pleasure in a foreign* language (Swarbrick 1998).) For examination purposes there are some similarities between reading in the target language and listening:

- Pre-listening exercises such as those mentioned in the previous chapter can equally be used before beginning to read for comprehension. Students can be asked to deduce from the question what sort of information is required, before actually trying to find it in the text.
- Reading is often used either to test students' overall knowledge of the language, or their acquisition of the most recently-taught structures and vocabulary. Some consideration needs to be given to the strategies which students need to develop in order to understand what they read.
- New concepts are often better reinforced through **non-authentic** reading material. A series of sentences to be grouped according to tense may be a good way to practise, for example, the difference between the use of the perfect and the imperfect in French. An account may be split by the teacher into sentences which are jumbled. Students are then asked to put the sentences into a logical sequence, perhaps using some suggested linking phrases. Such exercises go beyond simple reading for comprehension (once a passage has been read and – in the student's mind at least – understood, answering the questions can be quite uninspiring) to add an extra dimension which is at the same time purposeful and straightforward to complete.

However, there are some techniques which are particularly appropriate for reading. Acquisition of vocabulary (see Chapter 1) is at least as important for reading as for listening. However, the use of the dictionary in class- or home-based activities, which is of very limited value in listening because of the gap between sound and spelling, is much easier to manage in reading. On the other hand, while good use of a dictionary can help students learn new words, its over-use can turn reading from a pleasurable activity to slow drudgery. It may be good to have some ground rules to overcome this problem, especially for those conscientious students who like to get everything 'right', for example as follows:

- Read the passage right through (with the help of the questions, if any) before you use the dictionary at all.
- Use the **strategies for coping with unknown words** (see later in this chapter) before you use the dictionary.
- Use the dictionary for no more than (say) five words in any passage.
- Guess first; use the dictionary second. See how often you guessed right. (If the passage is at the appropriate level for the student, the proportion of correct guesses should be quite high).

In order to discourage over-use of the dictionary, the teacher might give students a **glossary** of words in a particular passage which he or she thinks may cause problems.

As there are different types of listening, so there are different types of reading:

- **Short factual items** such as signs, notices, advertisements. What is usually required here is the ability to extract details, often items of vocabulary. The question will often point to a certain kind of answer – time, price, date, etc.
- **Letters**. The student may need to extract specific details as above from longer sequences of the target language, or to understand the gist of the writer's opinions or points of view. In gist comprehension, it is often necessary to weigh up some seemingly contradictory statements in order to arrive at a conclusion. If the writer says: 'I can always talk to my mother, and my father is great fun, but my little brother can sometimes be annoying' and the question asks 'How does X get on with her family? [A very well/B quite well/C not very well/D badly]' the student can't really get to answer A without understanding practically every word, and then coming to a conclusion.
- **Hand-written letters**. In addition to whatever linguistic problems such a letter may pose, the handwriting of a native speaker can in itself be a barrier to comprehension. This is more of a problem, perhaps, in some languages than others, but if native handwriting contains some idiosyncrasies students need practice in recognising them.
- **Longer narratives and accounts**. Questions on these will commonly ask for both specific details and comprehension of the gist of a section or the whole. Clearly, such longer items are likely to feature more at the higher levels (Grade C and

beyond). If there is a number of questions about a long passage, this indicates that many of them are looking for specific details; it may be quicker and easier to work from the questions to the passage (see also the point about sequence in the section on exam techniques), identifying each piece of information as it is required. However, a small number of questions about a long passage indicates that it is necessary to understand the gist of the whole, or sections of it; in this case, it is vital to read the whole passage through first, to gain an impression of its overall meaning.

- **Newspaper articles**. The same principles apply here as to narratives and accounts, though there may be more non-linguistic clues. Pictures can help to indicate the subject matter – though it will never be possible to answer a question by relying just on the visual. Headlines, sub-headlines, the use of bold text can all be useful in identifying key points in an article, and may also give some guidance on whereabouts to look for particular pieces of information. On the other hand, the use of brackets, examples or statistics often indicate that the key point is made elsewhere.

What makes students want to read in the target language (TL)?

The simple answer to this question is probably 'whatever makes them want to read in their own language'. In any class of 30 learners, there will certainly be some who read for fun, some who read to find things out, and some who claim not to read at all! These distinctions are in themselves not at all clear-cut. Fun reading may be fiction, but is more likely to be the sort of magazine which features gossip about soap stars, tips on glamour and so on, while others would consider this to be reading to find things out (about soap stars, make-up, etc.). The group who don't read at all (often boys) may, on closer examination, read just as much as the others – but they often do their reading on-screen (teletext or Internet). Although it is hard to cater for the wide and unpredictable tastes of a whole class, it may be possible to motivate quite a large proportion some of the time.

- **Class library**. The wider the range of reading material available in the classroom, the more likely it is that individual students will find something they want to read.

There are a number of published reading schemes, sets of reading cards, etc. which aim to provide this variety. The very fact of being able to choose what to read is in itself a motivating factor, but it must be said that a set of 50 short class readers between a class of 30 students is probably not enough choice to satisfy all of them.

- **Language learning magazines**. These are excellent at providing a range of different types of reading, but this means that few students will be motivated to read everything they contain, and they are not easy to **categorise** (see below). In any case, because the cost usually falls on the student, they are mainly for the already motivated.

- **Extracts from TL newspapers/magazines**. These can be really attractive for students, but because it is necessary to be very selective of both content and linguistic level, they are often not very cost-effective in terms of price, and, perhaps more importantly, of teacher time.

- **Pages from the Internet**. These are relatively cheap, and are often on topics of interest to many students, but again a great deal of time can be spent in selecting appropriate pages. If the school is on-line, it may be possible for some students to do their own surfing on French sites, but a good deal of supervision would be needed, and one problem of seemingly suitable sites is the intensive use of slang, which often renders a page useless without a great deal of editing.

- **Teacher-adapted material**. This may be less appealing to students than 'authentic' reading (lack of illustrations, etc), and does take time, but may be the only way to rescue a piece which is generally very suitable, but which may be too long, contain too much slang or too much unknown vocabulary. This could also refer to the assembling of materials from different sources. A selection of headings where the article itself is too long and/or complex (a day's football results, for example) could form useful reading material. Even this kind of topical information can have a certain shelf-life, since *'Auxerre bat Lyon 2 à 0'* or *'L'Onu inspecte des sites militaires et nucléaires en Irak'*) are fairly timeless.

Once a wide range of reading material has been acquired, probably from several different kinds of source, students are more likely to be motivated to read it if it is well **categorised**. A brainstorm with the class can often come up with appropriate categories, and material can then be stored in the classroom under these headings, so that students can quickly find something to interest them. While students should be encouraged to read as widely as possible, it is certainly better for them to read willingly a lot of material on, say, sport, than to read reluctantly a few passages on a range of topics.

The element of choice of reading matter is enormously motivating, especially if it is not always accompanied by testing of comprehension. Although some practice of reading for detailed understanding is necessary preparation for the GCSE exam, this is adequately dealt with in most coursebooks, combined with some use of past papers, and is probably better kept separate from the idea of 'free' reading. Encouraging students to do a range of activities with their reading will give them a greater feeling of independence and more motivation. Some of the following activities have the added attraction of requiring little or no preparation by the teacher:

- presenting content visually (picture, cartoon, graph, diagram) – fact or fiction;
- summary of the content – fact or fiction;
- personal reaction to the ideas – fact or fiction;
- personal response (like or dislike) – fiction;
- comparison with the English situation, e.g. factual passage about TL customs;
- list of new information acquired – fact;
- development or continuation – mainly fiction;
- production of similar piece, e.g. profile of famous person;
- transformation, e.g. changing narrative to dialogue.

Although many of the above activities are probably better done in English – the focus, after all, is on reading – some students might be encouraged to do them in the target language. The later activities are only suitable for higher-achieving students.

Occasionally, of course, it may be appropriate for students simply to read, without any follow-up activity.

The process of selection, possible adaptation, and categorisation is time-consuming, but really pays dividends in terms of ease and desirability of use by students. Because of the time required, it is essential that this is a departmental activity, and that developed resources are shared.

How can students cope with unknown words?

There are a number of **strategies for coping** which students should be familiar with when reading in the target language. These are important in personal reading, as they can limit the use of the dictionary, making reading both quicker and more enjoyable, but they are vital in the Reading test, where the use of a dictionary is not allowed. Whenever they are faced with an unknown word, students should be encouraged to:

- look at the context, as they do in English. In the sentence *'The man had a large X on a lead'* it's easy to decide that the missing word is a breed of dog – which can then probably be ignored as far as comprehension is concerned. At least, using the context is a good way of checking any 'guesses' produced as a result of other strategies;
- consider similarities with English words. There are many target language words which have the same, or almost the same, spelling as in English. This technique doesn't **always** work (*assister* in French doesn't mean to help, but to attend) but it's worth trying.

There are many common prefixes (beginnings) or suffixes (endings) which can be added to target language words, and which are very similar to English: if the basic word is known, the meaning of the compound is easy to deduce, e.g. *inoubliable* – un**forgett**able. There are other patterns in French which, although they aren't similar to English, can help in understanding:

dé- in front of a verb changes its meaning to the **opposite**:
charger – to load   *dé*charger – to unload;

-eur at the end of an adjective turns it into a noun:
profond – deep   *profond**eur** – depth;

French words beginning with *é-* or *es-* often begin with 's' or 'es' in English:
étudiant – student; *espace* – space.

(AQA Specifications include extended lists of such *Communication Strategies.*)

What techniques are needed for success in the Reading test?

Advice for students

EXAM TECHNIQUES

All the exam techniques suggested for **Listening** are equally appropriate in **Reading,** as well as the following:

- Use the layout of the text to help (headlines/sub-headings/bold/brackets [often mean the information is just an example, so may not be crucial for gist understanding]/figures and statistics).

- Remember that questions will almost always be asked in the same order as the information appears in the text – except when the question is testing overall comprehension. This is also true for Listening.

- Don't spend too long on the early questions – if there's one you really can't do, leave it, and go back at the end (don't forget).

- Don't leave an answer blank, or resort to guessing, until you have tried the strategies for coping with unknown words (see previous section).

key points

- **Reluctant readers can be tempted to read if there is a wide variety of passages, articles and stories on topics which interest them, and if they can choose not only the reading material, but the activity to follow it.**

- **If they are to read well and easily, students must become aware of word patterns. They need to accept that they will frequently meet unknown words, but that there are ways of dealing with them.**

- **Reading does not have to mean books. Shorter, more factual pieces are often more stimulating.**

- **If all staff are on the lookout for appropriate reading material from whatever source, the MFL department's resource base will be built up much more quickly and easily.**

Entering students for GCSE

chapter 8

- ☐ What are the requirements for each tier?

- ☐ How can estimates and entry decisions be made as reliable as possible?

- ☐ How can students best be prepared for the exam itself?

What are the requirements for each tier?

There is little difficulty in deciding on the tier of entry for the best and for the weakest students. The Grade Descriptions printed in the Specifications make quite clear the qualities required at Grade A (Higher Tier):

- In Listening and Reading, candidates can understand gist and identify main points and details, recognise attitudes and draw conclusions.
- In Writing and Speaking, they can give information and narrate events, in longer sequences of the target language using a variety of structures accurately, and can justify opinions and points of view.

and at Grade F (Foundation Tier):

- In Listening and Reading, candidates can extract some information and identify some details.
- In Writing and Speaking, they can produce short sentences and substitute words and phrases.

In general terms, students who can satisfy the descriptions for Grade C:

- in Listening and Reading, are able to identify main points and details, including past and future events;
- in Writing and Speaking, are able to give information and express opinions using different tenses, conveying clear messages.

They will be entered for Foundation Tier unless they show clear evidence of at least sometimes being able to go beyond the Grade C description.

However, the situation is complicated by the possibility of different Tiers of Entry for the different skills. The following are some general guidelines, to be used with caution, since the performance of a given candidate on the day of the exam can be unpredictable:

- Students who never perform beyond Grade C should almost certainly be entered for **Foundation across the board**, since in most skill areas the Grade C threshold mark may in practice be more accessible on the Foundation paper.

- If it is thought desirable to give a borderline C/D candidate the chance of a Grade B, the 'easiest' of the higher papers is probably **Reading**.
- Students should not be entered for higher Writing unless they have shown **clear evidence** that they are able to cope with the tasks, and gain a number of marks on the higher tasks, as well as doing well on the overlap section.
- In Speaking, there is a considerable risk that the confidence of borderline candidates can be adversely affected during the test itself by poor performance on the harder role play(s), and that therefore their performance in the (more highly weighted) Conversation will suffer. Higher Speaking is a good option only for the better candidates.
- From the 2003 examination, there is no longer a 'cut-off' at the bottom of Higher Tier tests, which in the past has resulted in some candidates scoring 0 points because they failed to score within a few marks of Grade D. This means that entry for a Higher Tier paper no longer carries quite the same risk, though the problems referred to above which may result from over-optimistic entry remain.
- Although it remains statistically possible to gain Grade A* with one Foundation Tier paper, Grade A with two papers at each Tier, and Grade B with three Foundation papers, in practice, because of the very high scores required, such outcomes are extremely unlikely – for example, a candidate gaining A* including a Foundation Tier paper would have 'dropped' 9 Uniform Marks or less across all four tests.

How can estimates and entry decisions be made as reliable as possible?

Mock examinations using actual past papers are clearly one of the key ways of deciding whether students should be entered for Foundation or Higher Tiers in each skill, and of deciding on the appropriate estimated grade. To be of maximum value, these examinations should be:

- carried out under conditions as close as possible to those of the real exam. This is particularly important for the Speaking test;
- marked according to the mark schemes and assessment criteria used by the relevant examining group. These are available each year, and must be applied

rigorously if the resulting information is to be accurate. Even in Listening and Reading, 'made-up' mark schemes can give significantly different results. In Speaking and Writing, unless the principles of the assessment criteria are understood, marking will be very unreliable.

In the case of students for whom there is doubt about the appropriate tier of entry, it may be possible to provide 'combined' past papers which include the Foundation, overlap **and** Higher elements. A mark can then be given for both the Foundation and the Higher tests.

Centres which enter students for the written Coursework option may find the period set aside for mock examinations useful for the completion of the controlled conditions piece.

It is worth noting that in the unfortunate event of a candidate's absence from part of the exam through illness, a rigorously conducted and strictly marked mock examination may be accepted as good evidence of his or her level of achievement, especially if this matches the estimated grade. However, results in mock examinations are only one part of the evidence which needs to be considered when deciding on the tier of entry and the estimated grades. It is also important to bear in mind:

- **progress** which may be made by students between the mock examinations and the final exam. Predictions about this can be more accurate if the previous year's mock exam results are compared with actual GCSE grades within the centre;
- **the teacher's knowledge** of each student's abilities. A particular student's performance in a mock exam can be unexpectedly poor (for any number of reasons) or unexpectedly good (for example, if the past paper contained questions very similar to those contained in the coursebook). These variations may modify the impact of the mock exam result alone;
- **the department's knowledge** of the performance profile of the centre in previous years – though this of course may change according to staffing changes or conscious improvements in departmental policy.

In the case of a **new Specification,** for which past papers do not exist – the Specimen Papers provided by the examining groups are often modified by the time the real thing arrives – and for which an Award of Grades Meeting has not yet determined grade threshold marks, it is always necessary to give relatively less weight to mock exam scores (which may not be based on genuine past papers) and more weight to the teacher's knowledge of the student. An absolute principle which all awarding groups are obliged to adhere to is that of continuity of award – basically, that work which was of Grade C standard in the final year of a previous syllabus will continue to gain a Grade C in a new Specification. This means that experienced teachers can carry over their knowledge of what constitutes a particular grade, and use it in making decisions on Tier of Entry and estimated grades.

How can students best be prepared for the exam itself?

Although it is important not to over-emphasise exam practice at the expense of teaching, there is no doubt that, whatever their level, in order to achieve their full potential, students must be familiar with:

- the **different question types** used by the appropriate examining group;
- the **assessment criteria**. In Listening and Reading marks are simply awarded for providing relevant information, but in Writing (both Terminal exam and Coursework) students need to be aware of what they have to do to achieve certain levels on the criteria. Since the language of the criteria themselves is not often student-friendly, this means that they must be told in appropriate terms what the examiner is looking for (see Checklists in Chapter 5).

- Tier of Entry should be considered for each individual student. It is not necessarily (nor even frequently) the case that every student in a top set should be entered for four Higher tests.

- The mock exam should be as close as possible to the real thing, in terms both of administration and marking. This not only gives teachers the most valid evidence on which to base their judgments, it also avoids unpleasant surprises for students on the day of the final exam.

- The professional judgement of the teacher should be taken into account, as well as formal mock exam results.

- If students are to include in their Writing and Speaking everything they need to achieve their potential, they must be aware of what is required to attain a certain level on the criteria for assessment.

References

Adams, J. (2002) Pathfinder 35: *On course for GCSE coursework*. 2nd ed. CILT.

Adams, J. and Panter, S. (2001) Pathfinder 40: *Just write!* CILT.

Atkinson, T. (1998) InfoTech 3: *WWW/ The Internet*. CILT.

Berwick, G. and Horsfall, P. (1996) Pathfinder 28: *Making effective use of the dictionary*. CILT.

Brammall, G. (2001) *GCSE German vocabulary learning toolkit*. Collins.

Carter, D. (2001) *GCSE French vocabulary learning toolkit*. Collins.

Cheater, C. and Farren, A. (2001) Young Pathfinder 9: *The literacy link*. CILT.

Horsfall, P. and Crossland, D. (2001) *Vocabulary for GCSE French*. 3rd ed. Nelson Thornes.

Humberstone, P. (2000). *Mot à mot*. 3rd ed. Hodder & Stoughton.

James, C., Clarke, M and Woods, A. (1999) *Developing speaking skills*. CILT.

McLachlan, A. (2002) New Pathfinder 1: *Raising the standard*. CILT.

Snow, D. (1998) Pathfinder 34: *Words – teaching and learning vocabulary*. CILT.

Surridge, M. (1995) *Le ou la – the gender of French nouns*. Multilingual Matters.

Swarbrick, A. (1998) Pathfinder 36: *More reading for pleasure in a foreign language*. CILT.

AQA *GCSE Specification 2003* and *Specimen Papers*

Edexcel *GCSE Specification 2003* and *Specimen Papers*

OCR *GCSE Specification 2003* and *Specimen Papers*

Useful sources

Géo-Ado (43–45 avenue de Clichy, 75850 Paris Cedex 17)

Mon Quotidien (33 rue du Petit Musc, 75004 Paris)

www.canalj.net

www.eurosport.fr

www.french@yahoo.com

www.infojunior.com

www.momes.net

www.parcasterix.fr

Appendix 1:
German examples

Making longer sentences

From p19

Going beyond the minimum

From p51

Making longer sentences

und – and
*Ich sehe fern **und** ich mache meine Hausaufgaben.*

aber – but
*Ich möchte ins Kino gehen, **aber** ich habe kein Geld.*

dann – then
*Ich habe meine Hausaufgaben gemacht, **dann** bin ich schlafen gegangen.*

danach – next
*Erst wasche ich mich, **danach** frühstücke ich.*

der (die, das) – who
*Ich habe einen Bruder, **der** John heißt.*

wo – where
*Ich wohne in einer Stadt, **wo** es viel zu tun gibt.*

wenn – when
Wenn ich Zeit habe, höre ich gern Musik.*

während – while
*Ich unterhalte mich mit meinen Freunden, **während** ich mein Brot esse.*

weil – because
*Mir gefällt Geo, **weil** ich den Lehrer mag.*

was – what
Was mich in der Schule interessiert, das ist Geschichte.*

(das) was – what
Was ich gern mag, ist meine Ferien im Ausland verbringen.*

bevor – before
*Ich räume mein Zimmer auf, **bevor** ich mit meinen Freunden ausgehe.*

P © CILT 2003

nachdem – after
Nachdem ich gegessen habe, wasche ich ab.*

da (ja) – since
Da wir **(ja)** in die Stadt gehen, werde ich mir Zeug kaufen.*

wenn – if
*Ich werde nächste Woche ins Kino gehen, **wenn** ich genug Geld habe.*

obwohl – although
Obwohl ich Fußball liebe, gehe ich nicht oft zu einem Match.*

---

sehr – very
gewöhnlich/im allgemeinen – usually
auch – also
endlich – at last
(un)glücklicherweise – (un)fortunately
plötzlich – suddenly
oft – often
andererseits – on the other hand
dennoch/doch – however
einerseits ... andererseits – on the one hand ... on the other hand
normalerweise – normally
fast – almost
bald – soon
später – later
ziemlich – quite/fairly
vollkommen – completely
endlich/zum Schluss – finally
übrigens – besides
sofort – immediately
das heißt – that is to say
zum Beispiel – for example
auch – also
und so weiter – and so on

Going beyond the minimum

Ich bin fit.

➡ **Ich glaube, dass** ich **im Augenblick** fit genug bin.

Ich habe zu viele Süßigkeiten gegessen. Ich habe oft in Fastfoodrestaurants gegessen.

➡ **Als ich jünger war, habe** ich viele **Süßigkeiten gegessen, wie** Bonbons und Schokolade. **Dazu** bin ich viel **mit meinen Freunden** in Fastfoodrestaurants gegangen und war **deshalb** etwas dick, und ich war **überhaupt nicht** fit.

Jetzt esse ich Obst und Gemüse.

➡ Jetzt **habe ich** mein Diät **gewechselt,** und ich versuche Obst und Gemüse **zu essen** und **nicht zu** naschen. Ich gehe **nicht mehr oft** zu McDo.

Ich bin sportlich. Ich gehöre zur Fußballmannschaft in der Schule. Wir spielen jeden Sonnabend ein Match.

➡ **Ich bin schon immer** ziemlich sportlich **gewesen, denn** ich liebe Fußball und Schwimmen. **Jetzt wo ich** zur Fußballmannschaft in der Schule gehöre, die **im Augenblick** viel Erfolg hat, trainiere ich **dreimal**

in der Woche, und wir spielen fast **jeden Sonnabend** ein Match, also das genügt als (körperliche) Bewegung.

Ich rauche Zigaretten. Ich will wie meine Freunde sein. Das ist nicht gut für die Gesundheit.

➡ Leider habe ich im vorigen Jahr angefangen **zu rauchen.** Das hab ich getan, **um** wie meine Freunde **zu sein,** aber ich weiß wohl, **dass** das dumm ist. **Als** ich das letzte Mal Fußball spielte, konnte ich nicht laufen.

Ich werde nicht rauchen. Ich werde um elf Uhr ins Bett gehen.

➡ Ich habe **also** beschlossen, das Zigarettenrauchen sofort aufzugeben. Ich werde außerdem in der Woche **vor** elf Uhr schlafen gehen, **denn** ich bin im Unterricht oft müde, und wir haben bald Prüfungen. Also, ich **werde** sehr fit sein, nicht wahr?

Appendix 2
Spanish examples

Making longer sentences

From p19

Going beyond the minimum

From p51

Making longer sentences

y – and
*Veo la tele **y** hago mis deberes.*

pero – but
*Me gustaría ir al cine **pero** no tengo dinero.*

y entonces – then
*Hize mis deberes **y entonces** fui a la cama*

y luego – next
*Primero me lavo **y luego** desayuno.*

que – who
*Tengo un hermano **que** se llama John.*

donde – where
*Vivo en una ciudad **donde** hay mucho que hacer.*

cuando – when
***Cuando** tengo tiempo libre, me gusta escuchar música.*

mientras – while
*Hablo con mis amigos **mientras** como mi bocadillo.*

porque – because
*Me gusta la geografía **porque** la profesora es simpática.*

lo que – what
***Lo que** me interesa en el colegio es la historia.*

antes de – before
*Arreglo mi habitación **antes de** salir con mis amigos.*

después de – after
***Después de** cenar, lavo los platos.*

ya que – since
***Ya que** vamos de compras, voy a comprar un jersey.*

si – if
*Voy a ir al cine la semana que viene **si** tengo bastante dinero.*

aunque – although
***Aunque** me gusta el fútbol, no voy mucho a los partidos.*

---

muy – very
normalmente/por lo general/la mayor parte de las veces – normally
también – also
al final – at last
(des)afortunadamente – (un)fortunately
de repente – suddenly
muchas veces – often
por otra parte – on the other hand
sin embargo/no obstante – however
por una parte ... por la otra – on the one hand ... on the other hand
casi – almost
pronto – soon
más tarde – later
bastante – quite/fairly
totalmente – completely
finalmente – finally
además – besides
inmediatamente – immediately
es decir – that is to say
por ejemplo – for example
también – also
y así – and so on

P © CILT 2003

Going beyond the minimum

Estoy en forma.

➡ **Creo** que estoy en **plena forma en este momento.**

Solía comer demasiados caramelos. Comía muchas veces en las hamburgueserías.

➡ **Cuando era más pequeño, comía** muchas **cosas dulces, como** los caramelos y el chocolate. **Y además** iba a las hamburgueserías **con mis amigos, así que** era un poco gordo y **no** estaba **en forma.**

Ahora como frutas y verduras.

➡ Ahora **me he cambiado** de dieta y intento **comer** frutas y verduras y **no picar.** Ya no voy **mucho** a McDonalds.

Juego en un equipo de fútbol del colegio. Hay un partido todos los sábados.

➡ **Siempre me han gustado** los deportes, sobre todo el fútbol y la natación. Juego en el equipo de fútbol del colegio, que tiene mucho éxito **en este momento.** Me entreno **tres veces a la semana** y hay un partido casi **todos los sábados,** así que hago mucho ejercicio.

Fumo cigarrillos. Quiero ser como mis amigos. No es bueno para la salud.

➡ Desafortunadamente, el año pasado empezé **a fumar.** Lo hize **para ser** como mis amigos pero sé **que** es estúpido. La última vez **que** jugué al fútbol, no pude correr.

No voy a fumar. Me voy a acostar a las once.

➡ **Así que** he decidido dejar de fumar a partir de hoy. Además me voy a acostar **antes de** las once, **porque** muchas veces estoy cansado en clase y dentro de poco tengo exámenes. Así que **estaré** en forma, ¿verdad?

timeless topics for all MFL teachers

Classic Pathfinders deal with those MFL issues that will never go away. Based on the wisdom contained in the best-selling titles in the *Pathfinder* series, the material has been re-written and updated by the original authors in the light of the challenges of today's classroom. Each title contains re-editions of two related titles in the *Pathfinder* range which are truly 'classic'.

Classic Pathfinders are for:

- experienced teachers refreshing or renewing their practice – particularly as they go into positions of leadership and need to articulate the principles of good practice;
- newly qualified or beginner teachers who want to build up the essentials of good language-teaching methodology.

Classic Pathfinder 1	Classic Pathfinder 2	Classic Pathfinder 3
You speak, they speak: focus on target language use	**Challenging classes: focus on pupil behaviour**	**Inspiring performance: focus on drama and song**
Barry Jones, Susan Halliwell and Bernardette Holmes	*Jenifer Alison and Susan Halliwell*	*Judith Hamilton, Anne McLeod and Steven Fawkes*

classic pathfinder

the MFL perspective on today's issues

New Pathfinders

provide an expert MFL perspective on national initiatives. They are designed to support the language-teaching profession by ensuring that MFL has its own voice and ideas on the issues in education today.

New Pathfinders provide user-friendly support, advice and reference material for today's CPD agenda.

New Pathfinder 1

Raising the standard: addressing the needs of gifted and talented pupils

Anneli McLachlan

New Pathfinder 2

The language of success: improving grades at GCSE

Dave Carter

New Pathfinder 3

Impact on learning: what ICT can bring to MFL in KS3

Claire Dugard and Sue Hewer

new pathfinder